Teenie:

Newslady in Training

By

Steen Miles

Teenie:
Newslady in Training

By
Steen Miles

Orman Press, Inc.

Lithonia, GA

Teenie: Newslady in Training

By
Steen Miles

Copyright © 2007
Orman Press, Inc.

ISBN-13: 978-1-891773-84-6
ISBN-10:1-891773-84-4

Scripture quotations are taken from THE HOLY BIBLE, King James Version.

Printed in the United States of America

10 9 8 7 6 5 4 3 2 1

Orman Press, Inc.
Lithonia, Georgia

Contents

Foreword   vii

Introduction   ix

Dedication   xi

Chapter One   *The Beginning*   1

Chapter Two   *The Early Years*   18

Chapter Three   *Friends*   50

Chapter Four   *High School*   69

Chapter Five   *College Bound*   133

Chapter Six   *Love & Marriage*   141

Chapter Seven   *The Fourth Day of The Month*   153

Epilogue   167

Acknowledgements   173

Teenie: Newslady in Training

Foreword

My Dear Sister,

You have inspired us all and served as a wonderful role model in so many ways. I am glad to see your creative processes come to fruition with this insightful and inspirational book.

As the oldest of our 9 siblings, you taught us all that journaling is important. You began journaling as a child and have captured events in this book that will be a legacy for the children and grandchildren of our family and others.

God sprinkled you with the talents of reading, writing, and speaking. These talents began your illustrious career in Broadcast Journalism. As readers go through the pages of this book, which spans several decades, a number of emotions will be tapped—sadness, happiness, laughter, and sometimes anger.

You will find throughout the story that training up a child is not an easy task. However, there was a constant ingredient that has never changed and that is LOVE.

Love you #3,
Mary K. Sanders, Ph.D.

Teenie: Newslady in Training

Introduction

Teenie is the true story of the coming of age of a young African American girl whose parents, from a poor, segregated rural area of Mississippi, raised her in a white, middle–class northern Indiana neighborhood during the 1950's and early 60's. Teenie initially expresses her hurt and anger over racism, sexism, colorism, and classism by striking back at her tormentors. Her father, a Baptist minister, lovingly but firmly holds tight the reins on this wild, young colt, who by amazing grace is transformed into quite the thoroughbred. The reader is taken on a roller-coaster ride of emotions that will have you laughing, crying, and even angry as you experience the clash of cultures between the "Rev" and his strong-willed, first born, Teenie.

Train up a child in the way that (s)he should go and
when (s)he is older (s)he will not depart from it.

(Proverbs 22:6)

Teenie: Newslady in Training

Dedication

I dedicate this memoir to my loving parents, the late Rev. Austin and Rose Edna Davis, whose love and Godly guidance gave me the courage to meet life's challenges head on. I also dedicate this book to my wonderful siblings, for whom I have so much love, the late Austin Jr., Mary, Richard, Mae, Bruford, Philip, D.J., and Brad. My life has been given incredible meaning because of my beautiful friend–daughters, Kellie (Elderjoy), and Heather (Babyjoy), who encouraged me to write this long–overdue memoir. My precious grandchildren, William and Kellea, thank you for enriching my life. To my children's father, LeRoy King, Jr., thank you for loving me when you did and how you could, enough to make me your wife. To Robert Miles who cared enough to say "I Do, I Will, and I'll Try."

To childhood friends who played important and

I am because you are
and because you are, I am.

(West African Proverb)

invaluable roles in my life. For the teacher of all teachers, the late Elizabeth Greer, whose impact has lasted a lifetime. To my cousins/big brothers Jewel, Edison, J.W., and Paul Rogers; thank you for many life lessons, including boxing instructions. My late Aunt Alberta Davis Rogers, a teacher who was really a Queen and who was more like a grandmother than an Aunt. For Grandfather Albert Davis, the oak. To my Sister/Aunt, the late Lola Wheeler Gray who taught me style and grace. To my mentors, Misses Ellen Warren, Luberta Jones, Ruby Paige, and Mary Cherry; thank you for being the lights that illuminated my path to womanhood.

I pray that thousands of women, men, boys, and girls will read this book and gain the understanding that true self–esteem comes from the knowledge of God's perfect love for us and that true success can only be found in kingdom seeking first. Only He validates us. All beauty is from within, as we are made in the Creator's perfect image, for His glory and to embrace the brotherhood of all mankind. Enjoy these incredibly funny stories. I pray you will be blessed by them and find lessons I finally learned, albeit the hard way.

—Steen Miles

Chapter One

The Beginning

Who can find a virtuous woman? For her price is far above rubies.
The heart of her husband doth safely trust in her,
so that he shall have no need of spoil. She will do him
good and not evil all the days of her life.

(Proverbs, 31:10-12)

The story of Teenie, Newslady in Training, begins and ends at the church. It began one hot, second Sunday afternoon in August, during "big meeting" as revivals were called in rural Collins, Mississippi; the community otherwise known as Friendship. My future Dad, on leave from the Army at Camp Shelby, met my future Mom at the snow

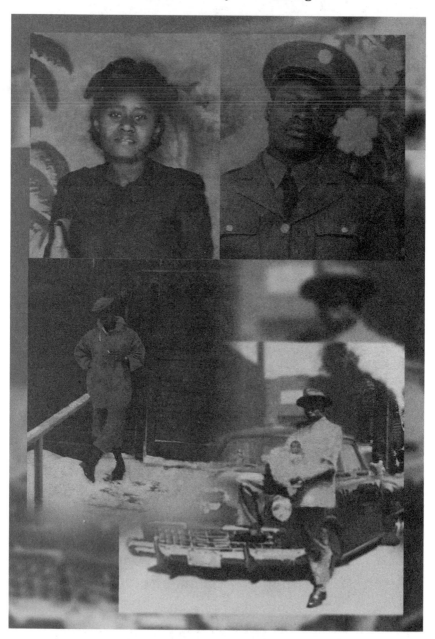

Mom, Dad—Early Days

cone stand on the grounds of Friendship Missionary Baptist Church. He was immediately taken by the petite, pecan-tan, doe eyed, 16 year old; with long black hair. Austin Davis, then 21, stood six feet, four inches tall and could best be described as tall, dark, and handsome. He was from Bassfield, Mississippi, or the Sweetwater Community about 15 miles away. Austin had inquired around and found out the young beauty's name was Rose, Rose Edna Wheeler. Rose was at "big meeting" with her grandmother Lucy Draughon, and her sister Lovie Mae, who was older by two years.

James Brown, not the famous singer, but a soldier also on leave from Camp Shelby, asked Lovie if she would like to go for a walk with him. According to my Mom, Aunt Lovie consented to go for a walk, but when my Dad asked my Mother to join him for a stroll in the nearby woods, she demurely declined telling him she would get in trouble with her grandmother if she left the church yard and indeed she would.

My great grandmother Lucy was a no-nonsense,

half-white, half Choctaw Indian a tiny little woman who could cuss up a storm. She was known in those parts as something of a root doctor who could go into those woods and find herbs and roots that after cooked up in a tea could cure all ills. Despite being a devout Christian, local folklore had it that my great grandma Lucy could also help get rid of an unwanted pregnancy with one of her teas. Rumor had it that she gave a white woman in the community one of her "teas" to end the woman's pregnancy. Folks say something went wrong and the woman died. But even on her death bed, she never told on Lucy. Don't know whether that's a true story or not, but Lucy's recipes for teas, good and bad, went to her grave with her at 106 years of age.

My great grandmother was some character. Her back bedroom at grandmother's house held a chifforobe with all kinds of withering herbs and a dried-up piece of skin that was supposedly a scalp! She was spooky. She was humped over, walked pigeon-toed, and stared at you with her big, cold grey eyes. She never married, but had three children; two by two different white men and the other by a married black man. One girl died at 12 of unknown causes. The baby by the married black man would become my grandmother, Christine Draughon (Magee) Wheeler.

In future years, I would look at Aunt Floydia Wilson and wonder, "Is she really my grandmother's sister?" My grandmother was fair-skinned, with long soft hair, but Aunt Floydia was a pure white woman with bone straight hair and grey eyes. Actually, she really had no African blood, just Indian, which in those days may as well have been black. In fact, the census records refer to my great grandmother as "Mulatto," and she had no African blood. Her father, John Draughon, was Indian and her mother, Parthenia, was white; one of the five daughters of Jackie Graves, all of whom married Indian or black men. Oh, the family!

My Dad had been married previously, but only briefly to a woman, described by the family members who would speak of such things; as a "fast"

Creole woman from New Orleans. The marriage was childless and apparently ended in divorce after only about six months. Now that was fast! But who could find a virtuous woman? My Dad had found his in the petite Rose; a pretty, quiet, church-going young virgin. In later years, Dad would often say that a woman could only give a man the gift of her maidenhead one time and what a precious gift it was. He was very proud of the fact that he was the first one to "know" my Mother—in the biblical sense of the word to know. He often spoke of how much he cherished her and their marriage. He would say no matter what happened, he would never leave her or his family—not until death; and it would take death for him to leave us.

Now back to the beginning. My Dad was completely smitten by the beautiful Rose. The long distance courtship was on. He began writing heartfelt letters expressing his undying love for her. My Mother said, "that ole tall, handsome, big foot soldier wrote the sweetest letters." She would spend hours slowly

6

reading them over and over. She liked him a lot. My Dad proposed to her by mail and said when next he was on leave he would speak to my grandfather. That was just fine by my Mom after all, she had finished eighth grade and for a girl in that era her education was complete. High school was like college.

Austin would soon come and ask Darncey Wheeler, my grandfather, for Rose's hand in marriage. On the appointed day, my father came with military cap in hand to plead his case. With my Mom peeking around the side of the house, Austin asked my grandfather if he could marry my Mom. Mom said my grandfather didn't mind really, but his older daughter Lovie Mae had just married James Brown and my grandfather didn't have anyone— as he put it, "to tote his water," since he had no well.

My Father offered my grandfather $100 dollars to dig a well and to marry my Mother. The deal was struck! My Dad had the blessings of my grandfather to marry his Rose for $100 dollars; the price of a new well. What a dowry! My Dad had essentially "paid for" my Mom.

All was well, except my grandmother was not pleased. My Father was too dark-skinned for her taste. Despite the fact that my grandfather Darncey was deep ebony, my grandmother and my great-grandmother showed little tolerance for darker skinned people. In later years grandma Lucy and grandma Christine would tell me not to marry someone as "dark as me" and have "all those little pick-a-ninny babies" that they would not claim.

As recently as the late eighties, my dear sister/ Aunt Lola, who was a mere eight years my senior, would remark how beautiful I might have been if my mother hadn't married my Dad! She often remarked how much better her children were received and treated in Collins because of their light brown skin tones. Poor Aunt Lola, she even made differences in her grandchildren based on their color. God has such a sense of humor. Each of her children married spouses of dark brown hue. Colorism! It's no small wonder that I gravitated toward my Dad's family, who were darker like me.

I felt such love and warmth from the relatives

on the paternal side of the family, especially from my Grandpa Albert, a tall stately original Free Mason who himself could not read or write but raised up teachers and preachers. Despite the fact that school was not available to him—born 19 years after the end of slavery—he always stressed the importance of education.

I will praise thee; for I am fearfully and wonderfully made:
marvellous are thy works; and that my soul knoweth right well.
(Psalm, 139:14)

At 17 years of age, not really young to marry in those days, my future Dad took my future Mother as his bride. He took her to his older sister Alberta's house where the marriage bed awaited. My Mother was a virgin and she was not about to let a man do "those things" with her. So as my cousins all peeked through the holes in the knotty wood framed house, they were doubled over laughing as my Dad begged my Mother to consummate the marriage. Nothing worked. Dad had to take my Mother home and talk with her mother, my grandmother. Lord, chastity was indeed a virtue in my Mother's eyes. She still thought babies came out of a stump hole in the yard!

My Dad soon had to return to Camp Shelby to be shipped out for more fighting during World War II. In later years, he would never talk much about his experiences, too unpleasant I imagine. He would say later that those men who bragged about what they did in the war were probably only cooks or never saw any action. Those who did see the carnage of war didn't relish talking about it. He was also at Camp Shelby when that horrific race riot occurred and hundreds of black soldiers were massacred. That too was something he never talked about. My Dad had a way of forgiving, forgetting, and moving on.

I press toward the mark for the prize of the
high calling of God in Christ Jesus.

(Philippians, 3:14)

My Mom and my Dad married on November 4, 1943,

10

at the court house in Collins, Mississippi. She would brag about being married three years before she had me, the eldest of their nine children. But always the curious one, in later years, I looked at my Dad's military papers and read where he was discharged from the Army on November 17, 1945. I was born August 20, 1946, nine months and three days later. They certainly didn't waste any time! My mother was as sweet and loving as any one person could be but she was a very unsophisticated country girl.

My cousin (big brother Jewel), eldest son of Dad's sister Alberta, tells the story of how soon after Mom and Dad were married, they were discussing his going into town to buy groceries. My cousins said Daddy had "big Army money" and they just knew Mom was going to reel off a list of all kinds of goodies that they could share. So when Daddy asked her what she wanted, Mom said, "Oh, I believe I'll have some peanut butter and crackers and a drink." That was some delicacy for Mom. Cousin Jewel said he and the others split their sides laughing at my unsophisticated Mother. Being very sensitive, she did not at all like them laughing at her and became very angry, storming off to their back bedroom at Aunt Alberta's.

One thing Dad did while still in the military was buy land. In 1944, he bought 40 acres in Bassfield and gave his father, Albert, lifetime tenant rights. Granddaddy could do anything he wanted to on the land, except sell it. In later years, Daddy would proudly show me the deed to "our land." Granddaddy would also say, "Hold on to your land." "They ain't making no more dirt." Not long after my Dad was discharged from the Army, he took his young bride and moved North, to the Promised Land— the land of milk and honey, streets paved with gold. No more poverty, no more segregation, plenty of opportunity. There would be major lessons the former staff sergeant would drill into me and my siblings. "Get an education and be a homeowner. Know how to do something. Make something out of your life. Don't have to sleep in a big fine car parked in front of an apartment and never forget where you came from."

I always wondered why Dad chose to settle in

12

South Bend and not Gary, Indianapolis, or Chicago; where most Blacks from Mississippi landed during the great migration north. Austin Davis was a visionary and from his military world view, he knew exactly where he was going and why. South Bend was home to Notre Dame University and Studebaker's, a thriving car manufacturer of the time. He could make a decent living for his new family and would have the opportunity for homeownership. From his view of the world, he knew a small college town would afford his family a better quality of life. The big teeming inner city, where many people lived in crowded apartments was not the life he wanted for his family.

Speaking of family, I was born early on a rainy Tuesday morning about one o'clock. The birth certificate says I was born in Memorial Hospital, but the fact is I was actually born at home and transported to the hospital—umbilical cord and all, atop Mom's stomach. Always the impatient one, Mom says I wasn't going to wait any longer for Dr. Mott to arrive, so I forced her to

Dad & Friends

kneel on a pallet of quilts and bring me into the world.

Speaking of doctors, there were only three black doctors in South Bend in the early years. Dr. Cassius Mott, Dr. Roland Chamblee, and Dr. Smith. Dr. Chamblee would later become a family friend. Dr. Mott was the family doctor and the only one Daddy would allow to treat him. Other blacks who had "arrived" would often tease Dad saying he was going to die going to that black doctor. They preferred white doctors. Daddy refused to be swayed. He had a black doctor and a black lawyer. He believed in supporting black businesses and often pointed to the Jewish community as an example of how blacks should support each other.

While Daddy seemingly embraced everyone and had many white friends at Notre Dame and in the local government, he was fiercely proud of our African heritage and did not believe in interracial marriage. He would often remark that birds of a feather flock together. To illustrate his point, he'd say, "Look at those birds sitting on that power line. The robins

Mom & Baby Teenie

and the bluejays can sit and roost together, but when it comes time to go to their nests, you'll never find a bluejay going home to a robin's nest unless it is lost."

Dr. Mott never made it, so the owner, Miss Marteen Chin, of the Southside rooming house where Mom and Dad lived was there to assist in the miracle of my birth. "Push, push!" She instructed Mom. Out I popped, an eight pound, six ounce female version of Dad. They named me Ollisteen, after my paternal grandmother, Ollie Belle; and my maternal grandmother, Christine. The spelling got changed a little to include the t-e-e-n from Miss Marteen Chin's name. My nickname immediately became "Teenie."

Chapter Two

The Early Years

After a few more months at Miss Chin's, Austin moved Rosie and Teenie to their first new home, a huge six bedroom, two bath, two-story home, located at 844 South Rush Street on South Bend's southeast side. There were three other Black families in the area north of Sample in those days, the Scruggs, the Brownes, and the Browns. The white people in the neighborhood stayed put and didn't move away because I guess the few of us didn't pose much of a threat.

My early childhood overall was good and extremely interesting; if not hilarious. One would be hard-pressed to dream up a fictionalized account of someone's life that could rival my true life experiences. My parents were products of the depression and were brought up in a very rural area of segregated Mississippi. Here they were bringing us up in a predominately white northern middle-class environment. There was an inevitable clash of cultures that would play out in major fashion.

Our home retained a southern flavor in food, manners, and life style. Elders were addressed as "yes ma'am" and "no sir." If they were old enough to be your parents, then you were expected to put a "handle" on their names, such as Mrs. Jones or Aunt Mary, and "Cudin" Woody. Under no circumstance did you call an elder by their first name only. Sundays, Wednesdays, and anytime the church door swung open, we were there experiencing the richness of the Black Baptist church.

This would all serve as a wonderful balance for me from the white world I maneuvered daily. I sang in the church choir, was treasurer for the Sunday school, active in Baptist Training Union; and often called on to

19

give welcome addresses and speeches for Easter and Christmas programs. Those "in-front of audience experiences" would serve me very well later in life. For the most part, my early years were happy. I felt loved and protected and there was never a doubt in my mind that my Daddy didn't love me. His most affectionate gesture was to go by and tousle my hair; it was a sign for me that all was right with the world.

What was not all right with my world were the bathroom and kitchen details. Another of Dad's favorite expressions was "Cleanliness is next to Godliness." "Your bathroom and kitchen should be the cleanest places in the house," he'd say. Being the oldest and a girl, the bathroom and kitchen details most often fell to me. I hated cleaning the bathroom and washing the dishes which we had to do by hand. I would try to pay my sister Mary to do the dishes when it was my turn. Mom would sometimes let us off, but no matter what time Dad came home, if the kitchen was not clean, and heaven forbid there were dishes in the sink, you had to get up out of bed and clean the kitchen. Mom would fuss and threaten to tell Dad on us, but Dad only had to walk into a room and look at us with his nostrils flaring and we'd fall all over ourselves trying to get the house straight.

We were never sickly children and rarely visited the doctor. During the winter months each week, Dad would line up the four of us single file and with an orange in one hand and a big tablespoon in the other and begin to dispense castor oil to us. He alternated the weeks. Castor oil one week, cod liver oil the next. That nasty castor oil prevented colds and probably any other malady you could think of. It was an awful tasting thick oily liquid that you would taste for hours when you burped. The cod liver oil was bad but not nearly as terrible as the castor oil. The smart thing was to immediately swallow, it and get a huge bite of orange to chase it. Poor Austin would invariably hold it in his mouth refusing to swallow, having it drip down his chin, and having to take more for wasting it. He never learned, even after weeks and weeks of having to go through the same ordeal. We were rarely sick and had few colds even in the frigid temperatures of "South Bend" winters. The castor oil regimen was Dad's way of showing his love for us. Who would have believed it? We sure didn't.

Daddy's love for us and the need to keep us warm went into overdrive during the winter months. Northern Indiana was the snow bucket of the world! All the snow that didn't hit Chicago was dumped on South Bend, which is located in a valley. The winters were harsh, but I don't ever remember a cold house. Sometimes there were snow drifts up to 10 and 12 feet high. We kids would dig a tunnel from the front door to the street, risking a suffocating cave-in. There was nothing quite as delicious as ice cream made with milk, vanilla, sugar, and freshly fallen snow—before the dogs turned it urine yellow. To come into our house from the outside was like stepping from an air conditioned hotel into the blasting furnace heat of a Las Vegas afternoon. Daddy kept that heat turned up to the maximum. We were not going to get cold. Some of my fondest memories were looking at our frosted window panes from the warm coziness of the house filled on a wintry morning, with the delicious smells of Mom making breakfast of grits, eggs, biscuits, bacon, and coffee.

Christmas caroling was another really fun time. Susie Carr's mother would give us the pitch with her little whistle and half a dozen of us—me the only chocolate drop amongst all that vanilla, would launch into "Deck The Halls" or "We Three Kings." The best part of caroling was getting inside from the snow with offers of hot chocolate or cookies from the people we'd serenaded. In those days, the *"kooks"* were kept locked up someplace because we never worried about someone harming us in any way or putting something into our hot chocolate or steaming hot cider.

For the first ten years of my life, there were four of us, Austin, Jr., who came two years after me; Mary, a year later; and Richard, 11 months after Mary. Two girls and two boys. A nice family, Daddy would say. He could take care of us without straining. Daddy was a great money manager. He bought two or three rental properties. I recall going with him on occasion to collect the rent. Dad was a bit of a financial wizard. The only new cars he ever owned were Studebakers, his first in 1948. After Studebaker went out of business, he only purchased two-year old Buicks or Cadillacs. "Let the other fella' take the depreciation. It's still a new car to me," were my Dad's famous words.

I was enrolled in Franklin Elementary School, which was a short walk through the alley from my house. It never dawned on me that I started elementary school two years before *Brown vs. Board of Education*; that 1954 landmark U.S. Supreme Court decision that made integration of public schools the law of the land. I didn't integrate Franklin, I just went there. It was normal. Whites and Blacks went to school together in South Bend at that time. Walking through the alley from my house was frowned upon for safety reasons and we had to take the longer route around the block on the sidewalk streets.

My teachers would invariably call me O-listeen, except for Miss Greer, my favorite teacher—my English

24

teacher. She said quite properly that when a vowel precedes two consonants it is pronounced with the short sound. Thus, Olli-steen. Her pronouncement stuck with me and to this day I correct folks with that same statement when they mispronounce my given name which is rarely used—except legally. Anyone who calls me Ollisteen or Teenie, goes way back. The other funny thing, every year, was trying to convince the registrar that my sister Mary and brother Richard were not twins. When school started, Richard's birthday on September 2nd, made him the same age as Mary until her birthday on October 4th. Since they were only 11 months apart, the registrar would invariably shake her head as if I didn't know what I was talking about.

For the first 11 years of my life, we lived on Rush Street. The other black families were the Scruggs, next door on one side; and the Browns, Mr. W.T., Miss Alberta, and Deloris. A couple doors down were the Browne's with an "e." Mr. Browne was nice, but Mrs. Browne was a fair-skinned snob who always threatened to call the police on us for getting on her grass. In my young mind the white families were nicer than she was. I was always sensitive to color and her meanness was because she was fair-skinned, I surmised, and she didn't like us just like my grandmother. In later years, I would end up married to her grand nephew! The police knew all of us. Mr. Scruggs got drunk and raised cane every Friday night. Mrs. Scruggs would take his paycheck and call the police. The police would come and haul him off to jail, where he slept it off over the weekend. He'd be back home Sunday night in time to go to work on Monday. Mr. Scruggs was really a very good hard-working man, who loved his family, and his liquor.

My sister Mary—number three of the four at the time—tended to wonder off every week, and every week the police would bring her home from two blocks away with what always looked like the biggest, shiniest, red apple in the world stuck in her mouth. Up on Sample Street, at the corner of Sample and Ohio; was Mac's Grocery. Mr. Mac, the only name we knew, was a Jewish merchant who extended credit to everyone in the neighborhood during the week. I'd often go and get my favorites, an orange "pop"—as we called soda—and a Twinkie cake. Mom or Dad settled up on Friday, payday.

South Bend was different from other big cities where Blacks migrated to from the south, at least it seemed so for me. The influence of Notre Dame was great. There appeared, at least on the surface, a genuine attempt to bridge the gap between the races. Our parents were proud homeowners, not apartment dwellers like the big city folk. "First generation haves," as I would later refer to them. In the early fifties, we had a "party line telephone," which meant at least three people shared a line; like neighborhood extension phones. You were on your honor not to eavesdrop on your neighbor. They could cut in on your conversation in an emergency. Still, having a phone was a luxury everyone didn't have in their homes.

Several times people would come over to watch our black and white television. Fewer people had those and whenever a Black person was on, we'd call out for everyone to come and see. Our house on Rush Street was also home to a number of relatives and other families getting their start. Daddy's Aunt Mary lived with us along with cousin Jewel, the big brother I never had. They were with us from the time I remember until I was at least 12 years old. The upstairs portion of the house was frequently rented out to families like Mary and Willie Cherry, and their children; then George and Hattie Mae Jones, and their children. From time to time, Thomas Randall and cousin J.W., also roomed with us. The house was always brimming with people and we just always seemed to make room for one more that needed to get on their feet.

He that hath a bountiful eye shall be blessed;
for he giveth of his bread to the poor.

(Proverbs, 22:9)

As far back as I can remember, the house would also be crowded with what was called "quartet" singers, rehearsing before their performances at South Bend's black civic theatre—"The Herring House" or local churches.

Daddy sang with a group called the "Evening Lights." One of my fondest memories is seeing Dad and the others in the group dressed in their *crème* colored suits, matching ties, with tan and brown cowhide shoes to match! They were very sharp and could really sing as they harmonized and slapped the side of their thighs to keep time. The tenors and the bass singers always stuck out for me. When they started tuning up, it seemed as if the house literally started rocking on its foundation. They would sing until the sweat rolled down their faces—to be mopped up with a big white handkerchief, which was standard to the uniform. The liquor seemed to flow as liberally as the sweat. I got in trouble for asking one time how they could be singing about God and drinking before they went to the concert! I must say though, I never saw Daddy take a drink, not then or ever. He said he just didn't like the stuff.

One evening, a rousing card game was going on in the living room. We had those aluminum based chairs with the padded vinyl seats and backs. This really heavy-set woman reared back in the chair to slam the table with the

Quartet Singers

winning card. As her considerable girth pressed against the chair, it flipped backward. The woman's dress flew up nearly to her waist, exposing her snuggies—those long cotton women's underwear that came down to the knees. Oh, it was a hilarious sight. We children howled with laughter until we were run off to bed, as we shouldn't have been up watching grown people in the first place. In those days, children stayed in children's places. When grown folks were talking or otherwise entertaining, you made yourself look scarce even if you were eavesdropping—which I would often do. Grown folks business was always far more interesting than the mundane happenings of us children.

In 1953, our household changed dramatically. Daddy accepted his call to the ministry. There were no more card games, gospel quartet singers getting tipsy, or big parties. When Daddy preached his first sermon at Mount Olive Missionary Baptist church, I, at the age of seven, "expressed my hope in Christ." I walked forward on my own, and said, "I loved the Lord and wanted to join church and be baptized." Rev. Tate stood me on the collection table for everyone to see. No one had prompted me, it was just something I was moved by the spirit to do. I've never regretted that day, even though there have been many times that I seemingly forgot that day. I thank God for never forgetting me asking to be His child.

The holidays were especially fun. It was a time for family and visiting. After Daddy became a minister, his life and ours changed along with his friends. A lesson he shared early was, "Short visits make long friendships. People running in and out of your house are nothing but trouble," he added. Christmas time was magical. To this day, many decades later, I wistfully reminisce and still miss the joys of Christmases past with Mom and Dad, my siblings, other family members, and close friends.

We children always had a few toys, some new clothes, and an abundance of food; ham, cakes, pies, fruit, and nuts. Even if there were not a lot of presents, there was always plenty of food and always oranges, apples, walnuts, and pecans. One big tradition was the "wedge,"—not a slice—but a large chunk of chocolate cake that Mom would leave out for Santa Claus, as I later learned was really for Dad. I always thought in my young mind, that it was no wonder Santa Claus was so fat because of the huge chunks of cake he ate! Christmas was a big deal, after all, we were celebrating the birth of baby Jesus. Austin, Mary, Richard, and I really believed in Santa Claus and would go to bed, scared to death to get out of bed or even peak out from under the covers because Santa would put ashes in our eyes, so we were told; and he wouldn't leave you anything for Christmas. We loved, but at the same time, were deathly afraid of that big, fat, white-man. When I found out there was no Santa Claus, it was pretty traumatic.

Dad was often away from home as a minister needing to tend to his flock. It was hard on Mom, she depended greatly on Daddy. With young children, Mom never really understood his need to be away from home and her so much. Being a Pastor's wife was not something she asked for, nor was she cut out for. Other women calling her husband, not knowing who was on the up and up and who wasn't. The slights and hurtful things people could sometimes say and do. There is an expectation of sin in the world, but it cuts to the marrow when the sin is in the house of the Lord.

Mom was never secure enough in her own right to fully understand how much Dad loved her. She was easily intimidated by whites and people in the church. Mom often remarked that people acted like they were "above" her. Daddy would tell me how much he loved her, but probably never told her. I don't remember him ever saying the words, "I love you" to any of us. He just tried as best he could to show it. For instance, Daddy would travel to Marshall Field's in Chicago and buy Mom all kinds of finery. Trips to Chicago were necessary for Daddy to find shoes to fit his size 14 quad E foot. He would also go to "Jew Town" to find the bargain Brooks Brothers suits. Gilberts, the only men's store that could fit his tall frame, was expensive. In retrospect, Daddy really was a first class kind of guy and always wanted the best for his family. I remember some really pretty shoes Daddy bought Mom that cost $96 dollars in the 50's! He loved his Rose, but like many men, he showed it in material things. Mom probably would have greatly appreciated more time with him. It seemed her frustrations were taken out on me, the first-born, and his female look-alike.

About 10 o'clock one Christmas Eve, when I was about nine years old, Mom took me to the bedroom closet to show me the clothes and dolls that my sister Mary and I were getting for Christmas. Mom said, "ain't no such thing as Santa Claus, me and your Daddy buy them things." I couldn't believe it! I went to get my sister Mary so she could see. When I asked Mom if I could see the toys and clothes again, she slapped me! I started crying. About that time Dad came home, "what's wrong with you?" He asked. "Mom hit me because I wanted to see our Christmas toys again." It was a rare moment of anger that I would seldom see from Daddy. He told Mom not to ever slap me again. "You whip these younguns behinds if they need it, but you don't slap them in the face or hit them about the head," he barked.

When we messed up to the point of needing a "whipping," Dad would never whip us if he was angry. He'd "save" it, he told us—for the next time. Funny thing, the white kids never seemed to get a "whipping," they got put on punishments. No such thing in our house. You did a crime, you were going to get a whipping.

Mom said Daddy was "shell shocked" from the war. I think Dad felt if he whipped us while he was angry, that he might hurt us. He could be so patient. Still to this day, learning there was no Santa Claus under those ugly circumstances, was a black day in my young life. Christmas lost its magic that night.

MISSISSIPPI

Summer vacations, any extended vacation, were always spent in Mississippi visiting relatives. Vacations in Mississippi always meant a fight between me and my cousin Hattie, the daughter of Daddy's sister, Aunt Alberta. Hattie was the baby girl of four girls and six boys, four of whom (Jewel, J.W., Edison, and Paul), lived in South Bend. During vacations, Cousin Glen Allen, the baby boy, and Martha Jean, the second girl; would always instigate something between Hattie and me even if it was no more than telling her that I was going to beat her up—which was not true. Cousin Augustine and I were very close. I looked up to Martha Jean and Lora Jean who were always in the kitchen with Aunt Alberta. But Hattie, she disliked me and for no good reason. She once told me how she hated to see me coming, "Talking all proper, wearing your little dresses and riding in ya'll's big fancy car." Mind you, in the 50's, most of my relatives in Mississippi still used mules and wagons for transportation, drew water from wells, used outhouses, and kerosene lamps. I loved the primitive and pristine countryside and never could understand Hattie's problem. Well, whoever started the fight, Hattie would be assured of getting her annual summer whipping. We stopped the physical fights by the time we were teens, but the verbal spats continued well into our adult years. I really loved her, but I was not going to back down from her; and since summer vacations were synonymous with Mississippi, we'd see a lot of each other. While I loved going to the country and seeing everyone, I vowed when I grew up, I would get a station wagon like the white kids parents with stickers from neat places they'd gone to on vacation; like the Smoky Mountains, Niagara Falls, and Yellowstone National Park. Every fall when we wrote themes about what we'd done for the summer, I always wrote about the great time I'd had in Mississippi; especially the boys coming to see me with their mules and wagons, busting watermelons in the field, and digging the "hearts" out of them; or trying to pick cotton. One day I picked 25 pounds of cotton. My Aunt Alberta and Uncle Javan, her husband, were just complimenting little Teenie for picking so much cotton. They were bragging on the little city girl. Hattie was furious. She could pick 25 pounds of cotton with one hand tied behind her and routinely picked 75 to 100 pounds a day! How she hated me. I learned later from my own misdirected dislike of a girl in high school, that hatred is a strong reaction to those we really envy.

School Days

I loved school, despite some slights, which were things like boys not wanting to hold your hand when time to get in a hand-holding circle. In retrospect, it probably had less to do with race and more to do with gender. Still, when it happens so frequently, the feeling is the same whether it's racial or gender discrimination. It still hurt to be rejected. There would be plenty more times. I felt so different most of the time and I was. When we were really young, classmates would ask if my skin could come clean, or "Why is your nose so flat?" I would tell them that I ran into the wall with my tricycle. I hated my big broad nose. I would put the clamp-type bobby pins on it every night hoping to make my nose thin like the white kids' noses. I sucked in my lips constantly so that they wouldn't be so thick and pronounced. Many years later, on several different occasions when I was

School Days

told I had a pretty smile, I was absolutely incredulous. The slights and hurts I experienced, I kept mostly to myself. My parents couldn't understand why I couldn't be deliriously happy. I was living in a great neighborhood with a nice home, nice clothes, and Lord, going to school with white children! They truly had arrived. I was the one who longed for others who looked like me.

Our neighborhood was a true melting pot, with Greek kids, Jewish, Italian, Mexican, Polish, and mostly White Anglo-Saxon Protestants (WASPS). There were plenty of fun times to balance the negatives. Like class with my first grade teacher Miss Tarnow, who looked just like an owl. How she could recite this poem called, *The Owl and the Pussy-cat.*

"The Owl and the Pussy-Cat went to sea
in a beautiful pea-green boat
They took some honey and plenty of money
wrapped up in a five-pound note
The Owl looked up to the stars above
and sang to a small guitar,

41

Oh lovely Pussy oh Pussy, my love,
what a beautiful Pussy you are."

—*Edward Lear*

Oh it was roll on the floor laughing time. We students would just howl. Imagine this woman who herself looked like an owl and in this shrill voice mouthing words which to many of us were very suggestive. It's an interesting dichotomy that the lyrics would be objectionable in class today—while so many other important standards of dress, speech, and behavior have been relaxed by today's mores.

Described as a very bright child, I recall sometime between kindergarten and first grade reading something that had the word pregnant in it. I phonetically sounded out p-r-e-g-n-a-n-t, pregnant and asked Mom and Dad what it meant. They just looked at each other. Well since they weren't going to tell me, I got the dictionary and looked it up. I confidently announced that pregnant meant a woman going to have a baby! Daddy just shook his head, not succeeding

42

in hiding his smile. He knew he had something on his hands. He'd have to work overtime with this one.

I also remember vividly the really ugly, brown, corrective shoes I had to wear in elementary school. My folks tried to make sure that I had pretty feet and that the arch support shoes they paid a small fortune for would counter the hereditary flat feet and bunions that ran on the Davis side of the family. But alas, several pairs of corrective shoes and years later, the bunions developed, the artificial arch had fallen, and the Davis feet were in full bloom.

Second grade would be a time of loss and instruction. The loss was felt when Donald, the only other black person in my class, moved away to the northwest side of town. I missed him so because he was my friend, he looked like me and he liked me. I could tell. One day in class when the teacher went around the room asking what our parents did for a living, some of the white kids were answering their fathers were accountants, lawyers, or other professionals. When it came Donald's turn, he said his father was a fireman, when in fact, his father at the time, hauled trash and wrote insurance. There was nothing wrong with either occupation, but Donald, like all of us; wanted to fit in and to do so meant embellishing his father's occupation. Self-esteem. In later years, Donald would end up marrying a white high school classmate.

It would seem the second grade was a pivotal time. Another unhappy incident occurred that began my "I'll show them attitude," when I needed to use the rest room. I didn't need to do number two, just number one, which was the numerical assignment for urinate. That's all I had to do. I raised my hand to signal the teacher for permission to talk and to ask to go to the rest room. She continued to talk to the class and ignored me. I raised my hand again whereupon she continued to ignore me. Finally I could not hold it any longer and wet my pants. My face was flushed hot with shame and humiliation as the other children—none who looked like me, laughed and snickered at the puddle underneath my chair. I had to walk home in the deep snow with the urine freezing on the back of my dress. Dad never missed an opportunity for a teaching moment. Checking his obvious anger that day, he told me that there will always be people who don't like you for whatever reason. "People won't like you because you're smart, because you're rich or poor, fat or skinny, wear nice or raggedy clothes. If they don't have a reason they'll make up one. Teenie, I want you to always remember that God loves you and to love yourself. It's not what someone thinks of you but what you think of yourself. You go back to that school and show that teacher who you are." Then ending the mini-lecture, others would be much longer; he pointed to his head and said, "If you get it up here, no one can ever take it away from you no matter what they do to you, and remember be the best you can be." To this day I don't know what my parents said to that teacher, but I made up in my mind that I would "show them."

But as for you, ye thought evil against me;
but God meant it unto good,
to bring to pass, as it is this day, to save much people alive.
(Genesis, 50:20)

I got my only paddling in the second grade, a result of an innate sense of curiosity that some might call just plain nosey, but it would also serve me well later in life—not in second grade though. Some boys were misbehaving at recess, which in those days was a 15 or 20 minute break from studies to allow students to play on the playground or just relax. Our teacher told the boys they were going to get a paddling once we came back inside. She told the rest of the class that we were not to look. In addition to recess in those days, corporal punishment was the rule of the day. A paddle was a thick slab of wood about a foot long that when well placed on the buttocks became a great deterrent to disrespect and misbehavior. Well we were told no one was supposed to look, but my curiosity got the best of me. While the rest of the class busied themselves with work or generally minded their business as instructed, I stuck my brown nose—the only brown nose in the class mind you, around the side of the door to look. Miss McIntyre called me out, "Ollisteen come here right now!" I was stunned. Incredulous, I asked, "How did you know it was me?" Poor child, but children really don't fully understand differences until they are pointed out to them. Needless to say, it was hard for the teachers to contain themselves from laughter as they gave me my soft swat for looking when we weren't supposed to. I guess I had a reporter's curiosity early on.

In all my years in elementary, high school, and college, I never had a teacher who looked like me. There were a few African American teachers in later years at my high school, but they were mostly confined to the junior high classes. Being on a college prep track, not many were assigned to us. It was as if black teachers could not teach college prep courses to the mostly white students enrolled in those classes. I believe many of these experiences had a negative impact on my self-esteem, despite my Dad's constant reassurances of my own self-worth. Teasingly, one day he told me I'd better get a good education because no one was going to give me anything. I looked like a little monkey, he said. I could have been crushed, but I wasn't. Boldly I retorted, "Everyone says

I look just like you, so you are the Gorilla who had me."
He burst out laughing. That child was too smart for her
own good. That's as close as one could get to talking back.

Now back to elementary school at Franklin, I had
a teacher who stood all of 4 feet 11 inches tall boosted by
her old black granny ankle shoes that she wore. She had
sky blue eyes with iron grey hair that was always in a hair
net. When the boys acted up in class, despite her tiny size,
she would grab them in their collar and shake them good
until their eyes bugged out. Today, she would be guilty of
abuse, and one of the finest teachers who ever went into a
classroom would be brought up on charges. Now, she never
had to shake me, because I was not a discipline problem. I
knew what awaited me at home if I dared waste precious
school time acting out. She always encouraged me. I
guess she saw my writing potential and would submit
my essays in competitions—I would win them. I also won
most of the spelling bees. At sixth grade graduation, I
beat out Frances and Sheldon and was the smartest kid
in the school. I had taken Daddy's lessons to heart. Be

the best. Show them. I was allowed the privilege of reading my so-called "valedictorian" speech at sixth grade graduation and guess who had to give me my certificates as I walked across the stage? You guessed it. That "ole mean teacher," who would not let me go to the bathroom.

Two teachers who didn't look like me; two distinctly different impacts. One would love her students. It mattered not whether you were black or white, rich or poor, she wanted you to be the best you could be. She and Daddy were singing from the same hymnal.

"A teacher affects eternity."

—*Henry Adams*

Chapter Three

Friends

I also learned something in second grade that should have been a harbinger of things to come. I wasn't smarter than my parents, especially Dad. At seven years of age, mind you, I thought no one else in the household could spell and I was already thinking about boys! In fact, I called my friend Geneva on our party line phone to tell her to be sure to come to my birthday party. "There will be some b-o-y-s's at the party," spelling out boys as parents do to children. Well dear old Dad heard me and said, "Teenie, get off that telephone. I'm going to b-o-y-your-s." He didn't use the term for donkey. In fact, in all my years of living with my Dad, I never heard him use a cuss word—Never!

Geneva was a good friend who lived a couple doors down on Rush Street. One day we got into an argument over what we were going to do. She ran up on her porch and yelled back, "nigger, nigger, nigger." Well always the fighter, I sicked my dog named Jitterbug on her. Jitterbug was a black standard cocker spaniel who would growl when my mother touched me. He was at Geneva's door in a flash and grabbed a mouthful of her behind. He just snarled and shook his head from side to side while holding on to her rear end. Geneva was hollering at the top of her lungs, "Mama!" Jitterbug really didn't hurt her, but despite that fact, her folks called the dog pound and they carried Jitterbug away. The dog that had been my lifelong companion was carted away and I never again saw him. Oh how I cried over Jitterbug. I was heartbroken. The painful lesson was that even though you are wronged and outraged, violence never results in anything good. It would be a long time,

however, before I fully embraced that valuable lesson.
I would have been able to continue enjoying my dog if I
would have ignored ignorance. Instead, I was wronged
twice. I was called a derogatory name and lost my dog.
There is an African proverb that says, "Never argue with
a fool. Someone observing may not know the difference."

"Sticks and stones may break my bones,
but names will never hurt me."

—*G.F. Northall*

It would be fifth grade before more blacks moved
into the Southeast side and came to Franklin as a
result of revitalization of the Southside. Finally, there
was another black person in my class. Johnny was
his name. He was a handsome guy, but the white
kids teased me and said he was my boyfriend; so
I avoided him like the plague. Besides, he gave no
indication that he liked me either, not like Donald.

One day, Miss Independent me, decided to go to the

movies. There was no one to go with me, so I decided to go alone. I got permission from Auntie, took my 35 cents, and took the short 10 minute walk downtown to the State Theatre on Michigan Street. I don't recall the name of the movie but it was a good one. God's angels, from the time I asked to be his child, have encamped all around me. I sat in that theatre watching the movie over and over. In those days you could do that. You didn't have to leave after the feature. I had gotten to the theatre around noontime. It was now nighttime and the family was frantic because no one had seen me. While munching on my third bag of popcorn, I hear a familiar voice softly calling my name in the dark. I turn around toward the end of the aisle and there was my mother, beckoning me to come to her. I asked what was she doing there? She calmly told me it was eight o'clock at night and no one knew where I was. They were worried sick. Strange, for the really big things I didn't get a whipping. For the little stuff, I seemed to get into trouble. Well, needless to say, I was never allowed to go to the movies alone. Can you image what might

FRANKLIN SCHOOL
5 A GRADE
1956 1957

Classmates & Family

happen to a ten-year-old girl alone in the movies today?

"All day, all night, angels watching over me my Lord."

–Unknown

My best friends in the elementary grades were Frances Lemanski, Geneva Lance, Julie Orban, Georgia Riakiatakis, Irene Theodosiou, and Delores Brown; an African American who lived next door—who was like the big sister I never had. Four years older, she didn't have a whole lot of time for me, but it was always quality time and I knew I could call on her to protect me from other "big sisters." As an only child, Delores had everything. A white French provincial bedroom, a television, and a phone— that she didn't have to share. This was in the early fifties. We had no idea how privileged we were when it came to material things. It became apparent to me only when we would travel south to Mississippi to visit relatives. In the fifties and early sixties, my grandparents still had outhouses, no electricity; and wells for water. It was like going to a foreign country—more on that later.

My friend Georgia was a Greek girl whose family was strict and orthodox. Georgia and I got into a fight one day, I don't recall what it was about, but she came closest to anyone to beating me up. She and another neighborhood girl by the name of Irene Ford, who also became my friend, could really fight. As the oldest, and a bit of a tomboy, it seemed I was always getting into some physical altercation. I never ever picked a fight; but I sure could finish one. Being at Georgia's house was so much fun, learning a completely foreign culture like the food and dancing. One odd thing, her parents were always listening to Italian music. *O Sole Mio* was always blasting from the phonograph. Sadly, Georgia and her family moved away, but another Greek girl came into my life named Irene Theodosiou. Irene came to Franklin in the fifth grade and she couldn't speak much English. Most of what Irene learned I taught her. We got into trouble playing in the Greek Orthodox church next door to where her family lived. I think her father was the caretaker. I learned some Greek words in exchange for my teaching of English. The

only word I can recall is "stoma," which means mouth—
probably because I had a proclivity for always talking.

The food and pastries Irene's mother
would make were mouth watering, especially the
Kourambiedes (wedding cookies), and Baklava.
Years later in Atlanta, I went to a Greek festival
because of my knowledge of the culture. As I excitedly
exclaimed that there were Kourambiedes, some
Atlanta matron looked at me and asked in her best
Southern twang, "Are you a gourmet cook?" I wasn't
dressed like a cook nor was I serving anything. I was
outraged and never attended another Greek festival.

In 1957, we'd moved from Rush Street to my parents
dream home at the corner of Garst and Main. It was a
big white house, trimmed in red, with a wrap around
porch; and a beautiful backyard flower garden. There was
a huge living room with a bay window and another bay
in the large eat in kitchen with a breakfast nook. Daddy
spared no expense it seemed in furnishing the house. We
had a huge floor model color t.v., sectional furniture—as

Mom called it, and wall to wall carpet. Relatives from Mississippi and friends from all over came to look at our beautiful home. This was a time I came to hate venetian blinds for many years into adulthood. The blinds in those days were metal things that could easily cut your fingers when you tried to clean them—pesky things.

There was another pest I'd have to deal with, the next door neighbor named "Butch." Butch was a thirteen-year-old menace to society. He was his widowed mother's youngest son who could never do any wrong. He was a sociopath of the highest order. What a brat! I don't believe he was a racist, just a spoiled, mischievous bigot; who would soon be taught a lesson he'd not forget. Soon after we moved next door to Butch and his family, Daddy's car would be—not so mysteriously—smeared with rotten eggs and tomatoes. One night, while I was giving a bath to my younger brother and sister, Richard and Mary; a brick came sailing through the window! Fortunately, no one was hit. I quickly ran to the window and swore I could make out a fat form running into the Hunt's back door.

One morning, a couple days later, we saw the culprit creeping back into his yard after pelting Daddy's car—it was Butch. Dad went next door to complain to Butch's mother about him and how her groceries kept ending up on his car. She defended her baby, "My son would never do anything like that. No, No, not my Butchie." The pelting continued until one morning I caught Butch red handed as he hurled an egg at Daddy's windshield. I ran and caught him and began beating his little fat behind until he looked like the "Pillsbury doughboy" smeared with strawberry jam. Butch went running into his house wailing with his bloody nose, "Mama, Mama." Well it wasn't long before his mother was knocking on the door with Butch in tow. Mom got Daddy who answered the door. "Hello," he said cheerily. Mrs. Hunt had no time for such pleasantries and huffily complained, "Your daughter beat up my Butchie, look at him!" Daddy fought back laughter as he managed to respond with contrived concern, "Who, Teenie? Not my Teenie, she would never do something like that. No, No, not my Teenie." The matter was settled that day.

Butch never ever pelted my Dad's car again. In fact, he made friends with my brothers. He had merely chosen the wrong way to introduce himself to his new neighbors.

Back to my friends; Frances was my best friend from kindergarten through sixth grade. I thought she was so beautiful with her long golden blonde hair and blue eyes. Frances was Polish and days spent at her house were a barrel of fun. Her father was never very friendly but her mother was like a model mother on the television commercials. Frances' mom was always in the kitchen baking or cooking one dish or another. The smells were great, but a lot different from my Mom's kitchen. From the Polish kitchen, was goulash and kielbasa, and other such goodies. Ours were fried chicken, pork chops, greens, and beans.

Frances was either at my house or I was at hers for most of those years. We traded sleeping over. Our only disagreements were about where to play in the wintertime. Frances liked to play outside with our sleds or make snowmen and such; I, on the other hand, wanted to be in the warm house having a tea party, playing with our dolls, or making doll clothes. She could keep the snow games, I wasn't interested. I now know that the inherent differences in our cultures were perhaps being played out.

I loved Frances like a sister. I remember her first communion which was such a huge deal in the Catholic Church. Frances wore this gorgeous white dress with all the ruffles and frills and they took loads of pictures. Her gown looked like a small-sized wedding dress. After all, she was marrying herself to the church. One huge picture of Frances in her communion gown graced their floor model TV. I thought that was really great. We had nothing like that in our church and I envied that part of being a Catholic. As a Baptist, I really couldn't understand, and frankly I didn't like the up and down on the knees rituals in her church. I couldn't understand anything, because in those years the mass was conducted entirely in Latin; and the huge savings grace was that they were done in a maximum 45 minutes. We Baptists, on the other hand, stayed in 11 o'clock service a minimum of two hours—

more depending on the dictates of the "Holy Spirit."

Frances was my best friend. Our birthdays were one day apart. We shared a lot of secrets about the boys we liked, walked home from school together, and were generally inseparable. Race is never far from the surface in this country, no matter how close kids are. Grown-ups find a way to muddy the waters. One day just before we graduated from sixth grade, Frances came over with an awfully dejected look on her face. "What's wrong," I asked. "Nothing," came the reply. Frances went on to say that she couldn't come over anymore. Stunned, as if she had slapped me, I asked why. She replied, "My dad said we are growing up and it is time we go our separate ways." I was drop kicked in the stomach, hit in the head with a sledge hammer, another blow to the self-esteem. There was no teaching moment here, just sadness on the part of both Mom and Dad. More on race relations would come later. That hurt I would just have to bear on my own.

"He'll be a friend to the friendless."

—*Unknown*

Friends

Frances and I both went to Riley Junior High School for seventh grade but we'd lost touch, we'd gone our "separate ways." My last name began with a *D* and Frances' last name began with an *L,* and since we were grouped alphabetically for homerooms, I never saw her again until we were both adults in our mid-twenties. We re-connected after she saw me on television and I invited her and her mother to my home for dinner. We have since exchanged birthday and Christmas cards each year.

Another hurt I'd have to bear on my own and had no control over was losing our big beautiful home. Studebaker's was falling on hard times and work was spotty. Daddy wasn't getting a big salary from the church like the mega churches of today and three more babies had come. Fortunately, we weren't set outdoors, but we had to downsize and move to a smaller house—a rental! It was on Fellows Street not far from where I'd spent the first eleven years of my life. By then, considerably more blacks had moved into the neighborhood. I did not like our house. It was decent by anyone's standards, but it wasn't what I was accustomed to. It had a dinky little kitchen, no dining room, only three little bedrooms for by now seven of us; and horror of all horrors, an oil space heater in the living room—no central heat or air! My brother Austin loved the fact that he no longer had to shovel ashes from our coal furnace at the big house. I was ashamed of this new place but soon settled in because I had no choice. I vowed then and there I would never ever be ashamed of where I lived again. I was still in the district and continued at Riley.

There were probably 100 blacks in the whole school of a couple thousand students at Riley, which was a combined junior and senior high school, grades seven through 12. My role model in those days was an upper classman named Verna. She was a dark brown skinned beauty whose family was one of the older families in the neighborhood across Sample Street, called the twilight zone. Verna was smart and had an enviable figure. She was active in school and dated this handsome football player named Alton. You rarely saw Verna without Alton. Their romance ended when she went to college in Atlanta.

Riley Junior High was pretty much uneventful for seventh and eighth grade. I maintained my good grades, sang in the school choir, and participated in school theatre productions under the tutelage of Mr. Cassidy; who split his time between Riley and Central high school. I was beginning to want to look grown up like my role model and wear straight skirts with the cardigan turned backward and buttoned down the back. But Dad had set down the rules, dresses would continue being the uniform for me and there would be no wearing of lipstick until age 14.

There were no school buses in the city because lines were drawn in such a fashion that everyone could walk to a neighborhood school. Only the kids in the county areas rode school buses. When the weather was really bad or when Dad had time, he would drop me off at school. The funny thing was he seemed to have an awful lot of time to take me to school. In retrospect, I think he was just making sure that I got there. Skipping school never ever crossed my mind, but I suppose a lot of kids did skip.

As soon as Dad would get out of view, I would whip

out my dime-store red lipstick, put it on, and march all grown-up into school. In the evening when he picked me up, I would have gone to the bathroom and used a paper towel to clean off the lipstick. Those coarse paper towels of the day still had wood splinters in them and my lips would be redder than the lipstick from trying to rub them clean of all traces of my new found cosmetics.

The Rev was soon on to me. "Teenie you been wearing lipstick?" He asked one afternoon. Busted! I couldn't lie. "Yes Sir." "I thought I told you that you had to wait until you were 14," Daddy replied. "I know, but all the other girls...,"—the absolute wrong statement. I learned that day two lessons; always tell the truth, and don't dare talk about what everybody else is doing. Telling the truth got me a reprieve and early permission to wear lipstick, a red color that he picked out! Always tell the truth. If you tell one lie you have to tell another one to cover up the first one. As far as what everyone else is doing, Daddy's stock reply was straight from Joshua—"for me and my house..."

On one of the nicer days when we could walk home

from school, a girl nicknamed "Yammie" started picking on me. It was always, I thought I was cute and that I talked and acted like a white girl. She made the mistake of pushing me. I proceeded to give her a good old fashioned whipping complete with a bloody nose. I beat her all the way to her house whereupon she ran inside and started throwing her mother's dishes at me. Everyone knew Dad, most black folks anyway. Yammie's mother called Dad to complain about me beating up her daughter. He said he would check into it. I told him about Yammie jumping on me and how I merely defended myself. I didn't even get my pretty dress dirty. For some reason, Daddy never chastised me or punished me for fighting. I never started a fight. I just finished them. It's been said if you want friends, first show yourself friendly. I tried to make friends but most often I was rejected. I didn't belong. Certainly not with the whites I'd grown up with, and most of the black kids said I was stuck up and talked white. What to do? Daddy's stock reply was, "Birds of a feather flock together and you are judged by the company you keep." Someone else said so profoundly: "Where you go determines who you meet, and who you meet determines how you think. What you think determines how you act and how you act determines what you do. What you do determines who you become."

Fight, fight, fight. That seemed to be the story of my life. I was the quintessential tomboy with frills. Walking home from school one day in the eighth grade, I got into a fight with a boy named Ben. He was walking behind me and threw glass at me, for no reason! Using the boxing skills I learned from my cousin, I beat him up. It's something we never talk about. He was too embarrassed. Hardy, always the antagonist, would remind him often that he'd been beaten up by a girl. Ben would go on to become a chief aide to a President of the United States! Thus ended two years at Riley for seventh and eighth grade.

Chapter Four

High School

The real fun would begin in ninth grade, in high school—South Bend Central High School. Here I was thrust into a social setting with more black kids than I'd ever been exposed to in my entire life. Central High School was in downtown South Bend. It drew from a number of feeder schools, mostly on the West and Northwest. Some of the black students like me came from predominately white schools and were tracked together in the college prep curriculum. Others from predominately black schools were tracked in general and slow learner curriculum—unless they were high achievers. I learned that fact many years later from my children's father, who also graduated from Central, six years before me. He came from predominately black Oliver Junior High School and said he never had some of the courses that I routinely took.

My first label came in the form of a question. "Who does she think she is?" For starters, Mom, as a child of the depression, and who said she never had lots of pretty dresses; wanted to make sure her girls did. "Rev. Davis, my girls going to look just as nice as those white girls," she would say when admonished by Dad about the amount of money she spent on our clothes. Each week she would bring home a new dress or two for me and my sister Mary. The dresses would most often be red, Mom's favorite color. No small wonder my sister later became a Delta. She had received many subliminal messages in those red dresses and coats.

My own personality was such that looking good was very important and I didn't want to wear the same run of the mill Lerner Shop clothes everyone else was wearing. As a secretary for the church, the little money I earned went to buying Bobbie Brooks outfits at Newman's and the Frances Shop—higher end stores in South Bend. I would lay away an outfit, pay it out the next month and lay away another one. I was some clothes horse. Even though I was told I had a great figure, I never wore revealing clothes; for starters, you weren't coming out of Rev's house that way. We couldn't wear shorts downtown, we had to dress properly. Pants were out of the question, except for a picnic or playing around the house. We couldn't wear pants to school, even in the frigid temperatures of "the Bend." If we wore pants or leggings to school, then we'd have to take them off, and put them into our lockers. That was a rigid part of the dress code. Here I was, well-dressed, smart, brown skinned with long hair, talking like a white girl! What an anomaly. I didn't grow up on the East side where all the elite, light skinned South Benders lived. I didn't grow up on the West side where the brown skinned elite lived. I didn't grow up on the Lake, which was the

71

far West side; I grew up in the white, no man's land of the Southeast side. I dressed, acted, and talked like a white girl! I was an unashamed product of my environment.

Ninth and tenth grade are challenging years for most. It was doubly difficult for me. Trying to find myself. Trying to fit in. Trying to be liked. Every day someone new was going to beat me up for no reason. I looked like an easy target. I had no cover. What those girls didn't know is that my cousin Jewel, a former golden gloves boxing champion, had taught me how to box like a prize fighter and I could fight. I knew how to block punches, throw a wicked right cross, and a left hook. I remembered well cousin Jewel's lessons, "Kill the head, the body will fall." Too bad for the girls who would hit me or challenge me.

In my freshman year at Central, a girl by the name of Myra and another girl whose name I don't recall were arguing and acting—in my lofty opinion—"ignorant" in gym class. "Miss Me" spoke up with an indignant air of superiority and asked them to please stop because they were making us blacks all look bad. Another lesson, mind your own business—you don't have a dog in that fight. Well, Myra, who was something of a Nubian queen in another life, about six feet tall and very dark, stopped arguing with the other girl and came after me. I stood my ground, repeating that she and the other girl were making us all look bad. Rightfully so, she asked, "What business is it of yours," and pushed me. Wrong move. I hit her with a sharp right upper cut to the chin and when she staggered back, I reached up and grabbed her by the neck and brought her down to a neutral level. I proceeded to pummel her. I threw her down on the gym floor and straddled her, all the while swinging left and right hooks. There was no scratching going on. Because Myra's hair was short, I took her by the ears and pounded her head into the gym floor. The gym teacher, Miss Matthews, pulled me off of her with the help of a couple other teachers and escorted both of us to the principal's office. We were both suspended for three days. Mr. Ferrell, the principal, asked if we could get home without anymore fighting. With my haughtiest air, I told him that I lived nowhere near her. Surprisingly, Daddy didn't say anything, but merely took me back to school after the three days. Myra was out for several weeks. She had no one to advocate for her.

Lesson: Never argue with a fool. Someone watching may not know the difference. A bright student full of promise had her record blemished by an unnecessary fight. It wouldn't be the last one.

Patricia, who was a light-brown skinned, really thin girl, made the mistake of questioning how I got my clothes; insinuating that I might be stealing them. Along with Connie, I was considered one of the best dressed girls at Central. Kids would gather at the big clock at Central every morning as a practice—but as an added bonus—they'd be able to see what Connie or Steen had on. By the way, it was during my Freshman year that I decided Teenie was too childish and asked my friends to call me Steen. It stuck, but Daddy and family continued to call me Teenie nonetheless. Someone told me Pat questioned how with so many kids in my family—seven of us by then—could I afford to dress the way I did. Pat came

74

from the elite folks on the West side and knew I wasn't one of them. Jealousy was obviously rearing its ugly head. I confronted her in the hall one day right after school. She had just left walking with her boyfriend, Lodis, a gorgeous, smart, tall, dark, and handsome football player who shared some classes with me. Pat was a year ahead. When I confronted her about her trashing me, she smarted off, and said, "well, how do you afford all those clothes?" Before I knew what hit me, I grabbed Pat, stuffed her into her locker, and slammed the door before strutting away. I was getting a horrible reputation. I was a prime candidate for anger management. Only in those days, there was no such counseling or at least I wasn't aware of it. Still, I was not about to let those jealous girls say mean, hurtful things about me, and get away with it. I'll show them.

For we know him that hath said,
Vengeance belongeth unto me,
I will recompense, saith the Lord.
And again, the Lord shall judge his people.
(Hebrews, 10:30)

One particular Saturday, while walking home from an afternoon downtown with my sister, a rather large white lady wearing shower thongs passed by me and Mary. I, the mischievous sort, laughed at the woman's dirty feet. I admit I probably provoked her reaction. I thought I heard her call me a "Nigger" but I wasn't sure. After walking a few steps I asked Mary, who was nonchalantly licking her ice cream cone, "What did that woman say to me?" Without missing a lick, Mary said, "she called you a nigger." "Let's go!" I said. We turned around and went back to confront the woman. "What did you call me?" I said to the lady. She stared me right in the face and repeated it, "Nigger, B—," as she proceeded to push me out of her face. Wrong move! Anyone who put their hands on me had trouble on their hands. I socked her a good one in the stomach. Being quite heavy, she didn't even flinch and responded with a swinging blow from her beefy arm that came from around her side and landed squarely on my jaw. The blow was delivered with such staggering velocity, I needed to quickly summon all the pugilistic skills Jewel had ever taught me. It was one of those Sophia,—from the *Color Purple*—punches that do some real damage. I gave her a fairly sound whipping that included a busted lip. The police officer who arrived on the scene broke us apart and demanded to know what was going on. I told him the woman called me a "Nigger" and she needed to know that this was not Mississippi. The officer, who was white, asked the woman if she had in fact called me a name. She admitted it. The officer sent us both on our way and told us to stay away from each other. What a different time.

When we got home, Daddy was doing what he did often; if he weren't reading the paper, he was reading his bible. This day he was reading his paper. The lessons about truth were at the forefront of my mind. I had to tell him somehow that I had been brawling again, this time downtown. "Daddy, what would you do if a white person called you a nigger?" "I would try to break their neck!" He responded. Oh what a relief. "Yes, Daddy, that's just what I tried to do." I then told him the story of the brawl downtown. I think Daddy realized his first born child was too much like him for her own good.

My need to be accepted by my own kind often got me in trouble. In my freshman government class, a boy named Roy asked me to write a note for him excusing him from class. Like an idiot, I wrote the note, got caught passing it to him; and nearly got suspended for forgery! After all, I did write his mother's name, just like he asked me. For some reason, despite the gravity of the offense, I missed getting suspended from school.

My best friends in high school were Brenda Hayes, Joan Lowry, Lynette Johnson, Betty Purnell, and Gelaine Waters. Gelaine attended Riley High School and was dating this guy who went by the nickname Bodie. Bodie was two and triple timing her. A girl from Adams High School liked him too. Bodie attended Washington High with this gorgeous football player named Al, who was supposed to be my boyfriend—even though I wasn't allowed to date.

After a Washington and Riley football game, at the stadium that we'd gone to, Eva who also liked or was dating Bodie, had challenged Gelaine to a fight. Well, I was instructing Gelaine from the sidelines how to punch out Eva. Gelaine was a quick study and quickly took care of Eva. That was on a Friday night. On Saturday, a girl down the street named Peggy, asked me to go downtown with her to get her mother some curtain rods. I told her I couldn't go—as Daddy had instructed me to stay home, but she begged me to go. Finally, I asked Mom who let me go downtown with Peggy. Peggy and I went into Robertson's Department Store, which was located in the heart of downtown on Michigan Street. I noticed some of the girls from the game the night before, they were East side girls; Eva, who Gelaine had beaten up, a toughie named Sheryl, and two sisters Lucy and Bobbie. When we came out of the store, they were waiting for us and started following us as we made our way the few blocks home. It was all a set-up and Peggy was part of the plot. Beware of so-called friends! Lucy was older and I learned later had a reputation as a real bully. She started walking right behind me calling me names and talking about my mother and father—who she didn't know. It was called playing the dozens, usually done by the guys. I kept walking and kept ignoring her. Finally Lucy made the foolish mistake of stepping on my heels. I turned around and asked, "Who did that?" She owned up to walking on my heels, called me the B—word, and pushed me. It was on! I slugged her in her jaw, and in the stomach, knocking her completely off balance and causing her to fall. I straddled her and began beating her with my fists as she clawed at me. She bit me on the inside of my forearm trying to get me off of her. I sunk my teeth into her forehead and took a big plug out of her head. Her sister Bobbie then jumped on my back. I bashed Lucy another good one before taking my gold-capped, pointy toed shoes, and kicked her while nearly impaling her on the spikes of a wrought-iron fence. No one else dared to get involved as I had decisively whipped two of the toughest girls in town.

My face was pretty badly scratched. By the time I got home, Daddy was home and wanted to know what happened to me. I told him about the six girls who jumped me downtown. Daddy called Lucy's father, a deacon in the church, to complain. Mr. Harris said Lucy told him she had run into the revolving door at the store and that's how she got the big plug out of her forehead. For the rest of her life, she carried a big "O" on her forehead as a reminder to never bother someone who's not bothering you. The lesson I learned: Watch your so-called friends. Peggy had set me up for those girls to beat me up. "Smiling faces, sometimes, pretend to be your friend." It was my last fight.

Training

Still, because of my strong-willed nature, Daddy and I were constantly at odds. He was determined that I would get a good education, not get pregnant out of wedlock, go on to college; and become a teacher. He was strict about school, being a lady, and cherishing your body. I couldn't take a course like home economics. He said Mom could teach me how to cook. "Take whatever courses those white kids are taking," he'd insist. I did. During several summers, Daddy would load up a bunch of kids and drive us up to Michigan for summer work picking strawberries. What fun. We were paid 25-cents a quart. We usually ate more than we picked but it was fun and we made a few dollars spending money. Those, I suppose, were my first lessons in earning what you wanted. He'd also take us on frequent drives to the south side of town to a street called Chapin Street. That's where most of the drunks and prostitutes hung out along a strip of clubs. We'd roll up our windows in fear of "those people" staggering down the streets cussing and such. Daddy would admonish us that if we didn't obey God's commandments and get a good education, we'd wind up like those people on Chapin Street. My Lord, what a fate! Many people who knew Dad before he became a minister, said he should not be so "old fashioned" and strict; that he should let me have more of a social life. Those same people who let their daughters and sons be "modern," ended up with bright futures snuffed out, many pre-mature grandchildren; and other problems. Ironically, those of us who were forced to go to church, and had parents with standards, ended up ok.

In those days, I did not understand. Everyone else, it seemed, could go to the dances after the football games. We called them "soc hops" because you danced in your stocking feet or in your socks. The dances usually lasted until 11 o'clock after the football games, which ended about 9 p.m. Well wouldn't you know, Rev would let me go to the game, but not the dance afterwards. He would always say "ain't nothing happening after midnight that is any good." Well, "little miss me" would sneak and go anyway.

Once during my freshman year my father had been in a bad car wreck and ended up hospitalized with a broken hip. I went to the football game and then sneaked to the "soc hop" afterwards. Daddy had made his customary evening bed check by telephone and found that I wasn't home. He had his police friends put out an A-P-B (All Points Bulletin) on me. Following orders, my mother literally took my picture off the wall to give to the police! I was deemed a missing person. Fortunately for Dad—the search began immediately, unlike more modern times of the nineties and beyond, when you weren't considered a missing person for 24 hours.

When I returned home about 11:30 p.m., Daddy from his hospital bed, instructed my mother to whip me. My brother Austin, took great delight in holding the phone so Daddy could hear Mom whip me. Mom started swinging the switch that I had to go and pick. I started crying, not very loudly, she wasn't really hurting me all that bad; but Daddy said she wasn't whipping me well enough because he couldn't hear me crying loud enough. He then instructed my brother Austin to tell Mom to whip me harder. Austin Jr. ended up becoming a career police officer. No small wonder because he was always the family cop! He was always spying and telling everything he knew and some of what he didn't. Still, my brother, though two years younger; was my protector and my friend. A guy had to come through Austin to mess with his sister.

It was clear that Daddy was obsessed with me getting pregnant. I think it was his biggest worry. It was no small wonder, I was talking about boys in the second grade. Dad did not give himself credit for doing

84

a good job rearing me; nor did he give me credit for being a decent young lady who just wanted to have a normal social life. Still, fearing I would somehow get pregnant while he was not present to watch me, he convinced the doctor to allow him to leave the hospital early.

The very next week, after the phone whipping incident, hard-headed me went to the game and went to the dance afterwards. When I got home again about 11:30 p.m., the Rev was waiting for me. He told me to bring a switch and he proceeded to whip me from his prone position—lying in the bed. I danced around the bed a couple rounds and decided enough. I'm not taking another whipping, so I took off running. This is a true story without embellishment. Imagine Dad, at 6'4" with a thin cotton robe, grabbing his crutches, and with his switch in his hand; hopping down the street after me with my Mom, my brother Austin, sister Mary, brother Richard, sister Mae, and Bruford and Phillip—all running down Fellows street in hot pursuit. I'm looking back yelling, "I'm not coming back. I'm tired of not being able to go anyplace and getting whipped." Austin, who stuttered when he got excited, said "O-O-O-lliste-steen you, you better co-come home. Yo-you-re crazy!" "I'm never coming back," I shouted. There was an older neighborhood guy home on leave from the Air Force who I thought was the most handsome guy, his name was Leroy (not the one I later married), and he saved the day. Daddy enlisted his help and Leroy caught up with me in his car after the family had abandoned the chase. By then I had run about three miles almost to Riley High School. Leroy drove alongside me and told me that my Dad promised he wouldn't whip me again if I came home. I came home. The house got quiet and there were no more whippings, not until next year, my sophomore year.

In the meantime, vacations were still in Mississippi. My freshman year was one of the scariest of my life going to Mississippi. It was 1960, and the freedom rides were beginning. We would invariably be stopped driving a nice car with northern plates and a clergy tag. Mississippi lawmen would shine their flashlights into the car to see who we were. I was always grumbling that Daddy didn't have to take that stuff from these men. We didn't do anything. Teaching Moment: You can be dead right. Daddy said, "I've got to allow these police to think I respect them so I can keep your Momma and y'all safe." Daddy would bend his tall frame so as to not tower over the little red faced, pot bellied, stereotypical southern cops; who routinely stopped us. Daddy would feign respect and say "yes sir and no sir" and inform them that he was taking his family to Bassfield to see his papa. After shining the flashlight into our sleepy eyes, and seeing nothing but shoe boxes with chicken bones and cake, they would finally let us pass. There were no restaurants to eat at along the way and black folks always had a shoe box lunch with fried chicken and cake to eat when you got hungry. There also had to be room in the trunk for an ice chest filled with soft drinks to wash it all down and to quench frequent thirsts in the searing heat.

There is no doubt in my mind that if all the black and white folks down in Collins, Mississippi weren't kin, and if I were a male child, I could very well have ended up hurt or killed like Emmett Till; a 14 year old boy, who like me was visiting Mississippi from up north. They claimed he whistled at a white woman and as a consequence, beat him beyond recognition, burned his body before anchoring it to concrete, and tossing him into a river. It will forever be etched in the annuls of history as one of the most heinous hate crimes to ever occur in this country. Those were dangerous times. I was always outspoken and verbal about the indignities of the colored bathrooms and other separate inequities. The colored bathrooms, we were forced to use, were invariably filthy. I would not use them and Daddy would not buy gas where we couldn't use the bathroom.

On one of our trips, Daddy, me, Aunt Mary, my sister Mary, and brother Richard were returning home in the winter of 1960. I was driving our car, a forest green Cadillac. As I was driving through Ripley, Tennessee, something happened to the transmission. We managed to get to a gas station. What normally would have cost $20 to $25 at home was going to cost $95; a lot of money in those days—a week's salary in fact. Daddy called Mom to wire the money. It was going to take two or three days to fix the car. There were no hotels for black people so where were we going to stay? While we were at the gas station learning what was wrong with our car, a white gentleman approached Daddy and offered us the use of his apartment, which was around the corner; so we could freshen up and eat until we knew what we were going to do. He pointed out a store close by where we could get some cold cuts, bread, and drinks. As we were going up the stairs to the man's apartment, I noticed the lace curtains part slightly at the window of the ground floor apartment. We weren't in the apartment a half hour before there was a loud banging on the door. "Police, Open up!" We were all in the kitchen and the apartment owner was sitting in his front room. He opened the door to be greeted by a red-faced beefy police officer. In a stern voice, he asked what was going on here. The apartment owner said he had invited us to come and rest while we learned about our car. The cop said, "You know we don't 'low nigras in white folks houses down here, both of you are going to see the chief." Well, it seems the chief and the entire police force were in the front yard of the house. After a few choice words, as a minister and a mason, Daddy was apparently able to diffuse the situation to the extent; however, that we had to leave the man's apartment. Daddy was able to find a fellow minister who directed us to a rooming house for the first night. That rooming house was awfully busy during the night; so we moved for the second night into to a funeral home where we spent the next two nights. We learned later that the female undertaker had a body, but she didn't want us to know because we'd have been too scared. The funeral home was, as you can imagine, beautifully appointed and immaculate. Just the place for a final resting place as we left Ripley, Tennessee, and an experience indelibly etched in my memory. For many years Daddy kept that funeral director's card in his wallet and always sent a Christmas card. I was out of school for an entire week. Everyone was worried about me, white and black kids. "Ollisteen, we heard you were stranded in Mississippi, are you o.k."

We were o.k., but would never be the same. I never knew segregation except for what I saw visiting my relatives, but I knew intimately discrimination. In retrospect, I rather think that segregation is not as debilitating as being led to think you're equal only to learn you are not. Daddy would make sure you didn't get it twisted. "Come here you young'uns," he bellowed one evening. "Listen." Lift Every Voice and Sing, he sang the lyrics in his strong baritone voice. He began to teach us the Negro National Anthem by James Weldon Johnson. "This is something they won't teach you in school," he said. He was right.

Other lessons that wouldn't be taught in school were taught at home by the Rev, some lessons by direct lecture, other lessons you learned from his actions. An example of a direct lesson occurred one day as he was driving me to school in the rain, I was grousing about a friend who I'd loaned an outfit to who hadn't returned it. In those days, wearing each other's clothes was quite acceptable, although it was not a practice I indulged in. I did loan my clothes but I was stopping the practice. I grumbled to Dad this particular morning because my friend hadn't returned the outfit in time. I said to Dad that's why I'd rather deal with white people. Dad said, "you see that gal crossing the street in front of us." I looked through the rain streaked windshield to see a young white girl. "As hard as she might try, she will never love you like your own kind. Don't you ever let me hear you talking about your own people that way."

Dad would always use the Jewish community as an example of brotherhood. "You never see a hungry Jewish person. When one comes to town, they all get together to make sure he has everything he needs. You never hear them talking about each other in public— remember that," he said. "And another thing, don't be so quick to make fun of somebody who doesn't have the material goods that you have." Remember, "There but by the grace of God, go I." Yes-sir! I got the message loud and clear. This was the same man, who bent low his 6'4" frame down in Mississippi and said yes sir, no sir, to a cop who stopped us for nothing. Situational ethics is a lesson I would soon learn. Always pick your battles.

That lesson would be played out one morning as Daddy was driving me to Central High. Some man cut in front of us almost causing Daddy to veer off the road. Daddy said, "Teenie, hold on, you're going to be late for school this morning. " In a flash, Daddy sped off and caught up with the man. In a couple strides, Daddy was out of the car, yanked open the driver's side of the car, and pulled the man out of his car by his collar. By this time, the man was sputtering and red-faced. Daddy said, "did you see how you nearly ran me and my daughter off the road? I will kill you." The poor man trembling said, "Leave me alone or I'll call the police." Daddy reached into his back pocket and pulled out his auxiliary police badge and said, "I am the police." Daddy shoved him back into his car and told him now get out of here and drive like you've got some sense.

Another teaching moment, beware of a black man without a mustache, and beware of a white man with one. Now just what that had to do with the road rage incident, I do not know except the white man had a mustache. While as a much exposed and enlightened adult, I've tried to move beyond that sage advice; it's still really hard. I always cast a second glance at a white man with a mustache.

All of these hilarious incidents are occurring while Daddy is in the ministry, either pastoring or as an assistant pastor. After finally accepting his call to the ministry— which he said he was reluctant to do—Daddy enrolled in and graduated from Bethel Bible College in Mishawaka, Indiana, a little town adjacent to South Bend. He received a high school diploma while in the military.

I don't know how families as large as ours made it with only one bathroom in those days of the 50's and 60's, but if you didn't get into the bathroom on a Saturday night before Daddy, you could forget it. He would be in there for hours, bathing, shaving, and then reading the bible. The toilet was made for other chores, but in our house, it was Daddy's throne on which many a Word came forth. The bathroom became his study.

Daddy's first church was Mt. Calvary located out on the West side on Washington Street. There was heavy foliage around the back of the storefront building. One evening during Wednesday night prayer meeting, Auntie, Daddy's paternal Aunt Mary, who lived with us, had to really call on the Lord. While she earnestly sang, "Father I stretch my hand to thee...no other help I know," from someplace in the back of the church a big wood rat lumbered its way toward her. When the rat saw all of us, it started scurrying and ran right beneath Auntie's seat, right between her feet. Auntie was fit to be tied. It would be the second time I saw those long cotton drawers called "snuggies" exposed. The theatre style seat Auntie was sitting in flipped up. Both her knobby knees jetted up in the air as she shrieked, "Aw s—t Jesus!" I thought I was going to get a whipping or die I laughed so long and loud. But because everyone else was laughing I didn't get in trouble. There were some really emotional prayers sent up that night, especially from Auntie, begging the Lord's pardon for her profanity—using the Lord's name in vain.

Mt. Calvary taught me a lot of lessons about the less-than-holy nature of some church folk. There was one know-it-all deacon by the name of Roger Blake who got kicked off the deacon board for the bad habit of helping himself to some of the money in the offering plate. He got caught stealing out of the benevolent fund. Perhaps it was that kind of bad habit that led to the practice in more modern times of having several people or counters tally up the offering in the presence of an armed guard. Deacon Blake was a short man, nearly bald with big bucked teeth that had large gaps between them which made him whistle when he talked. Every time he prayed it was "Lord, I thank you that the bed I slept in last night was not my cooling board." One Sunday after the announcements were read, Mrs. Fleming ended with her customary, "Please govern yourselves accordingly." Deacon Blake stood up and pronounced quite matter-of-factly that he was "DE-formed" of one of the announcements. I burst out laughing. He should have said he was "IN-formed" of the announcement. From his seat in the pulpit Daddy gave me a really stern look, but it didn't last long because even he couldn't help but fight back laughter. Mt. Calvary was a stereotypical black Baptist church of the 50's, but the spirit was always high. The women folk and and an occasional male would be "shouting" all over the church. There was plenty of fanning and falling out. We could always tell when Mom was getting ready to shout, because her knee would start bouncing really fast. Next thing you knew her arms would be flailing, and the purse flying, whereupon my brother Austin would always be in position to catch the money bag.

If ever there was a man called by God to preach, then it was Daddy. He could sing and he could preach the Word, but he also lived it. Always out helping someone, giving an individual or an entire family a place to stay, and feeding Notre Dame students—all the while taking care of his own family. He always modeled God, family and community. I would later come to realize those trips to Mississippi were strategic. Those trips were part of teaching us who we were and how to get in touch with our roots and families. He modeled "whose" we were but he could use a lot of help in the area of non-violence. I guess he was a lot like the biblical Peter. One day sitting in my 10th grade study period, I opened the newspaper to see a picture of a black man on the front page. On closer inspection, I see the headline: "Rev. Austin Davis Fired at Portage Township." Daddy was in charge of the office where families got government issued food and checks. In those days, the men had to perform community service work in order to receive the checks. Daddy supervised this operation as part of his responsibilities. Some subordinates were not treating the men with dignity on a particular job and were making derogatory comments to the men. Daddy had them reprimanded. They in turn complained to the county and Daddy was fired. He refused to back down—appearing to side with the recipients. The story made CBS evening news with Walter Cronkite! Daddy told them, as long as he was in charge, the men would be treated with dignity. They were already down and they would not be disrespected. Daddy went on to announce that since they'd fired him, he and his family would now be on public assistance.

My initial embarrassment gave way to an overwhelming sense of pride. Wow, my Dad was some heck of a guy.

After about ten years at the helm of Mt. Calvary, Daddy was named assistant pastor at New Salem Baptist Church, one of South Bend's largest. When Rev. Johnson left New Salem, another minister was called to Pastor. I think that hurt Daddy especially since he was the acting Pastor for so many months. He was later called to pastor Community Baptist Church in Elkhart, Indiana, a town about 16 miles away from South Bend, where he remained until his tragic death in 1968.

Daddy's best friend was Rev. Kirk. They were like brothers and our families were close. The Kirks' oldest daughter Billie Ann and I met in a near-fight over my brother Richard—who was always running his mouth about something. She threatened him and he ran to get me. I think we rather sized each other up and decided it wasn't worth seeing who was the toughest. We became great friends.

The Kirk's home was the only place I was allowed

Dad & Rev. Kirk

to spend the night other than with family. Mrs. Kirk was quite the character and she reminded me of my great grandmother. She was always dressed to the "nines" with her hair pin curled just so. Mrs. Kirk was the first preacher's wife I ever knew who smoked and cussed while regularly referring to the folks in the church as a "bunch of hypocrites". She also thought Mom was too soft and let those "biddies" run over her. Mrs. Kirk wasn't about to take any stuff from anybody. I was rather intrigued by Mrs. Kirk, but preferred something between her very earthy style and my mother's shy retiring style. Mom and Mrs. Kirk tolerated each other but Daddy and Rev. Kirk were like brothers. Rev. Kirk was a dignified, patrician type; the opposite to Daddy's gregarious humorous style. For many years Rev. Kirk pastured Laymen Chapel C.M.E. Church. In later years, he became pastor of St. John Baptist Church following the death of another of Daddy's good friends and mentors; the Rev. Bernard White. Daddy's role model was Rev. Charles Rowlette, pastor of Pilgrim Baptist Church.

I came to learn a lot about preachers and pastors sitting in on some of the ministerial alliance meetings while taking notes for Dad. At times, it was as if they forgot I was there. Rev. White was a short man with spectacles, whose language could get a little salty. He pastored one of South Bend's largest churches, St. John. One of the funniest scenes ever was at the trial sermon of a young minister at Rev. White's church. The young preacher was giving it all he had and not having much of an impact. The church was deathly still, hardly an amen. He was not an orator by any stretch of the imagination. Daddy and Rev. White were sitting in the pulpit with their oversized handkerchiefs stifling laughter, saying alternately, "Help him Lord." "Have mercy Lord." Later, I called Daddy on the exchange I'd seen between him and Rev. White; Daddy just admonished me to "hush" in between his side–splitting laughter. Rev. White and Daddy agreed, "that boy could not preach and needed a lot more practice." But what Daddy demonstrated publicly was who he was at home, a decent, God-fearing, family–

oriented servant who wanted the best for his family and community. He did not drink or use profanity, but he smoked like a chimney. Daddy sat me down one day, for one of his many lectures on life, and admitted he'd had an affair early in his and Mom's marriage. I was astonished! He told me he couldn't even remember the woman's name. He then went on to say, "If you think your husband is going to sit around you 24 hours a day seven days a week, you're sadly mistaken. Don't ever leave your husband because of something out in the street and beware of people bringing you news about your husband. What you must expect is that your husband will respect you, provide for you, and protect you and your children." Then came the lesson that really stuck with me and I've often repeated. "Get yourself an education. Prepare yourself just in case of the three D's—death, divorce, or desertion. You don't know which one is going to occur and you need to be able to take care of yourself and any offspring you might have." Lord, I was Daddy's laboratory project in training up a child.

Daddy taught me and Austin Junior to drive at

age 12 and 10 respectively. We were on our way home from Mississippi, just before we got to that huge bridge over the Kankakee River, Daddy gave me the wheel to cross over the Mason–Dixon Line from the South to the North. I held the car in the road on that two-lane bridge, but I was petrified. There was nothing but this huge expanse of water on both sides of me. Austin didn't take to driving naturally. In fact, years later when he became a police officer, we would tease him about his driving and wondered how he would manage in a high speed chase.

Daddy would let me drive to Church on Sundays and to the store in the neighborhood. When I got my beginner's permit at 15, I already had a car; it was a 1957 Ford Fairline 500—green body with a white top. It was sharp and I was the first girl in my group to have a car. My friends would ante up 25 cents a piece and we would ride for what seemed forever. Daddy told me, "When some joker says come go with me, I'll teach you to drive, or I'll let you drive my car; you can tell him you know how to drive and you've got a car!" Talk about a preemptive strike or getting ahead of the game.

My days of having my own car or car independence came to a screeching halt in my Junior year. Dad allowed me to take my car to my high school sorority club meeting. The Tri-Alphas was an elite group of young ladies sponsored by the Urban League and a lady named Miss Mitchell. Only the smart girls were members. I was proud to be one of them. Off to club meeting I went with best friend Brenda in the passenger seat. Always pushing the envelope, I didn't come straight home from the club meeting but went to our favorite hangout, Bonnie Doon's; a drive-in restaurant out on Lincoln Way West on the Northwest Side. Everyone was there, Mike, Lodis, Hardy, Ben, BoBo, Turtle, Gloria, Sugar, Beverly, Connie, Seifert, Jeanne; just about everyone who was anyone at Central. We were just hanging out having fun, playing the latest tunes on the jukebox, and drinking our malts— not liquor but sundaes. When it came time to leave, Tom, a white boy from my home room sees my car and challenges me saying, "It probably looks better than it rides." Wrong answer! Before I knew it, Tom and I are drag racing down Lincoln Way West at about 10 o'clock at night. Fortunately there was no traffic. The sidewalks tended to roll up at eight o'clock in South Bend. Tom moved in too close to me, and to avoid him hitting me, I lost control and side–swiped a car before rocking back in control. There was no damage to my car and I went on home without stopping. I hadn't been home long before the phone rang. It was the police, the tag had been traced to Dad. Dad was told his car had side–swiped a car on Lincoln Way West, a State Farm Insurance agent's car! The agent was working late and heard the noise. I don't know what happened. Daddy didn't talk about it. Two days later my car was gone and I never saw it again. From then on, when I was eventually allowed to drive alone again, it was to church and church only. Lesson: For every action there is a consequence and disobedience always leads to trouble. My wings had been clipped. Some things you don't know are wrong until you do them. My sophomore year in high school would become all knowing, at least I thought.

In the integrated setting of Central High School there were many interracial relationships, especially among the black guys and the white girls. Michael, my good friend whose Dad gave me my first piano, was an item with Barbara; a really sweet petite blonde that he'd gone to elementary school with. By now I was re–united with my friend Donald who'd attended Central and was dating a white girl named Sharon; who he subsequently married. There were precious few white guys openly dating black girls—except for a few brave souls like David. David and I were in Drama Club together. He'd given me his class ring and we were, I guess dating so to speak, since I really couldn't date—like going out with a guy. David and I would see each other when we could at school. An opportunity presented itself one evening for David to bring me home from a cast party following one of our productions. David and I were sitting out in front of my house which was a "no-no". Cardinal rules, no one blew the horn for you to come out of the house, they came in to get you; and you certainly didn't sit out in front of the Rev's house with a boy—a white boy? Lord have mercy, I must have taken leave of my senses. David and I were sitting there when Dad drove up. I immediately told David good night and went into the house but not before Dad had seen David's light brown straight hair in his headlights. Dad started his lecture. This was not a calm one. He was very angry! "Don't you ever let me catch you with one of them again. White men been raping black women for 400 years, don't you ever bring 'one' to my door again." I was shocked. My Dad, who had many white friends, and who would often give counsel to the Mayor and police chief, was a bigot? I think I had really gone crazy. I shot back. "I can't help it if you grew up in Mississippi and were subjected to all that racial abuse. If you didn't want us to have white friends why did you move into white neighborhoods?" I can't even imagine that all the horrors of the lynchings, the burnings, and other atrocities that Dad witnessed in Mississippi were now swirling in his head. Plus, I was sassing back. He lost it. The first and last time he would ever whip one of us when he was angry. He snatched off his belt and grabbed me and started beating me. I jumped up on my bed and started screaming at the top of my lungs that I was not taking any more whippings. I grabbed my radio and smashed it on the floor—not crazy enough to try to hit Dad. While he was momentarily distracted by my insanity, I took off running. This time Daddy wasn't on crutches and he took off after me. In three long strides he caught me and proceeded to whip me some more. A neighbor boy down the street, came upon us and begged Daddy not to whip me anymore. Daddy regained control and we went home.

The next morning, Daddy took me to school. When the folks under the big clock, where we all gathered, saw Rev striding through the halls headed to the principal's office; they wondered what had Steen done now? Daddy went right to Mr. Ferrell's office and demanded to see him. He announced to Mr. Ferrell that he was returning this boy's ring, that he was sending his daughter here to get an education, not for any of this social integration mess; and if this was the kind of school he was running, maybe he needed to see the school superintendent. That was the end of me talking to a white boy. White boys off limits, the black boys wanted the white girls or the fair skinned girls.

"If you're white you're right, If you're brown stick around.
If you're black get back!"

—*Big Billy Broonzy*

One afternoon while everyone was gathered in the cafeteria having lunch. Hardy, a boy I'd known since my days at Riley Junior High School called out my name. Hardy, like Mike, Lodis, Ben, and John were all members of the Top Cats; a group of black athletic and academic stars. In the crowded lunchroom Hardy yelled out, "Hey Steen, you sure are fine! But, you are too black for me"—to hoots and howls of laughter. I was hurt and humiliated, but fought back tears and tried to laugh it off as I made my way out of the cafeteria before the tears spilled. I know now that Hardy, who was much darker than me, was speaking from his own self-loathing, something too many of us had been made victims of. But the racism and the colorism would be far from over.

I had been a cheerleader at Franklin and Riley Junior High. But while the basketball and football teams at our integrated school were predominately black, there would only be one black cheerleader out of a squad of six. As athletic and as good as I thought I was, I lost out to girls who were lighter brown. It hurt. My grandmother's words would haunt once again—Rosie's "little dark kids." More hurt would occur when it came to the coveted queen's court for basketball. Following the balloting one morning in our junior year, several girls were saying congratulations to me as we passed classes; apparently knowing that I'd won a place. That afternoon however, when the list was posted, I was met with bowed heads. I had been replaced by a homeroom friend of lighter hue, who was nice, but not nearly as popular as me. More hurt. In later years, I had to do some self-evaluating. Could it be that it was not color after all, but class that got me taken off Queen's court? After all, I hadn't behaved like a queen in previous years what with fighting all the time, even though "I didn't start them," and was merely defending myself.

Lesson: Everything can't conveniently be assigned to exterior forces. We must always look inside. But there were balms, Daddy allowed me to go to two Senior proms my sophomore year. Not bad for a girl who couldn't date. Charles was my boyfriend of sorts. Since I couldn't date and wasn't "available," Charles was seeing a couple other girls. But when it came to his date for the prom, it was me hands down. He bravely came over from across town and asked Dad if I could go to the prom with him. Dad told Charles no, that I was too young. Charles, dejected, left and walked about a block, then turned around and returned. He asked Dad if he could speak to him again. Dad, curiously, said "Yes." Charles said, "Rev. Davis you don't want to spoil my senior prom do you?" Dad puzzled said "no, son why?" Charles said, "If I can't take your daughter to the prom, I'm not going; and this is a once in a lifetime deal." Dad looked at him, not believing that the young man had so much nerve. Dad gave him permission to take me but he

Charles & Steen

must have me home before 5 a.m., giving ample time for the after prom party. Truly amazing! We had a great time and Charles was the perfect gentleman in every sense of the word. He was not about to incur the wrath of Rev. Davis.

Mom loved Charles; he also worked at this new restaurant called McDonald's after school. Charles would always bring her some of those "little hamburgers." Charles moved to Chicago after graduation. Just as well, Daddy said he was a nice guy. His mother was really sweet but his Daddy drank too much and Charles had a big head. Daddy laughed and said with my big head and Charles' big head—if we were to get married, our children would have really huge heads. Perhaps it was just as well that Charles moved away, he was really a great, respectful guy. My other prom date was a guy named Lee. He was a neighborhood boy who would not have had a date, except that Dad let me go with him. I had a great time at both proms, except for a white girl having my exact same dress. We laughed about it. I complimented her on her good taste. We both thought by going to an expensive bridal shop instead of a department store that we would avoid any look-a-likes, oh well.

Other Lessons: My friend Phyllis lost her mother in our sophomore year. It was a devastating time for her and I wanted to go over to her house when all the other kids were going to help console her. Would you believe that tyrant of a father of mine would not let me go? Dad told me that everyone would be going to see Phyllis now, but she would really need a friend after the crowds were gone. It would be years before that realization would set in. It is now a mantra. Be there for your friends when the crowds are gone and short visits make long friendships.

Speaking of friends, my best friend Lynette got pregnant in the eleventh grade. Hardy was the father. Daddy said Lynette and I could no longer hang out because she was a mother now, and according to Dad, we had nothing else in common. "Birds of a feather, flock together." Teaching moment. "If you let someone get you pregnant," Dad said, "you'll be stuck rocking the baby while they go off to college and marry some nice girl." Lesson learned, "I would not be left rocking someone's baby."

JUNIOR YEAR

My junior year would bring more stability for me; I wasn't fighting anymore. The bullies by now knew that I was not for target practice. My grades were good, I was very much involved in school life, and I was coming into my own. I was a high school page reporter for the South Bend Tribune, our local town newspaper—a harbinger of my life ahead. As the Secretary of the Spanish Club, we had to conduct our entire meetings in Spanish. I became fluent in Spanish. I wanted to study several languages because I really wanted to be a United Nations interpreter or an ambassador and travel. Being an airline stewardess wasn't an option in those days. The only professions open to women in the early to mid sixties were teachers, nurses, or social workers. I was a cadet teacher—which allowed me to spend mornings in the classroom and afternoons at some elementary school doing practice teaching. I sang in the school choir and was a student council representative. I worked on the Junior Prom Committee and was also a member of the American Field

Service, which brought foreign students to study in the states. Our foreign exchange student, Ruthie, was a nice Jewish girl from England. We became great friends and remained in contact over the decades. We'd ride around in my car yelling, "Oh The Beatles" as we snapped our fingers to *It's Been A Hard Day's Night.* We had such great fun! I even picked up a clipped British accent.

The hilarity between my Daddy and me was far from over and neither was the hurt. Take the trip to the state basketball semi-finals for example. My best friend Brenda and I got the rare permission to go out of town to the basketball semi-finals at Ft. Wayne, Indiana, about an hour and a half from South Bend. I say rare permission because Brenda's mother, a divorcee, was nonetheless as strict as my father. Brenda and I were supposed to take the bus, which to us was oh-so-square. We had made other plans with John P., so we had Daddy drop us off early at Central's campus; which covered a half square block bordered by three streets. While letting us out on the Washington street side Daddy remarked, "Teenie, I

117

don't see the bus or the rest of the kids." "Don't worry about it," I offered. "We're early. You can go on and leave." I apparently still thought that I was really smart and my Dad was really that dumb. As soon as he let us out, Brenda and I ran through the courtyard to the Colfax side of the school where John P. was waiting in his Oldsmobile for the trip East. Seniors Lavelle and Edna were already in the car. We were all just friends. Brenda and I were home free, or so we thought. John P., as we called him, drove the two short blocks to the Western Avenue Standard Oil gas station to fill up. While he was pumping gas, there came a thumping on the rear passenger side window. Lord have mercy! It was the Rev! "Teenie come on out of that car," he bellowed. "You ain't going no where; Brenda, you can come on out too because you lied to your mother." Those were the days when everyone took responsibility for everyone else's child and ordered them about just like they did their own. Oh yes, it was a village. Oh but the shock, the horror, the surprise, and the humiliation. There would be no trip to the basketball semi-finals for us. Brenda's mother, who was always putting her on punishment did not deviate this time and put Brenda on punishment for a whole month. I surprisingly got lucky and was only lectured about doing what you say you are going to do, why riding the bus was a safety factor and not about control, or a lack of trust. I certainly hadn't behaved in a trustworthy fashion. Still, I was allowed to go to the finals in Muncie the following week but I had to ride the bus. I dutifully rode the old square bus which as it turned out, really wasn't so bad. Actually, it was kind of fun. I got to go out of town to the game to watch our powerhouse Central Bears battle Muncie Central. It was a cliff-hanger. We came in a heartbreaking second place in the state finals. Basketball was Hoosier hysteria in Indiana. In my yearbook that year, Brenda wrote, "Until the day I get too old to smile, I'll always laugh about the time the Rev caught us on our little merry way to Fort Wayne. You know what, I'm glad he caught us, but I learned one lesson and believe me, I would never try to fool him again, (smile)." On a completely different page in the

119

yearbook, John P. , who was driving wrote, "We had a nice time in Fort Wayne, too bad you couldn't make the trip. Best of luck when next year's tournament rolls around." The basketball trip and the Rev was a memorable moment in time that none of us would soon forget.

While on the subject of basketball, the captain of our team was a guy named Michael, who we called Mike, he was a good friend. His mother was my chief role model. She was a tall, pecan-tan, perfect size 14 with long hair. She was an immaculate dresser who always displayed an air of self-confidence. Mike's mom was active in the school PTA and was one of the few black parents who was not at all intimated by the white parents. She was a joy to watch. She always seemed particularly fond of me as well. I loved her style and wanted to be just like her. Please understand that I loved my own Mother and respected her, but Mike's mom had that certain *je ne sais quoi* that my Mother hadn't mastered and had no desire to. I was very fond of Mike, but, who wasn't? But I think knowing I was not his type, fair-skinned or white, I was

120

content to be his friend. Mike was always a really nice guy. He never lorded his popularity over anyone or acted in any fashion like a "jock god". He was our first Black Senior Class President, a sharp dresser, and just a really all-around class act. A new girl had come to town who was dating Recie, one of the Top Cats. Recie, who attended Washington High School on the far west side of town, was perhaps the only member of the T.C.'s who did not attend Central. Puddin was having a house party which was so very popular at the time. I wanted to go. Daddy said no because it was on the West Side and he didn't know "those people." Mom wasn't going to let me go either. Sometimes, even though Dad said no, Mom would let me go if I begged long and hard enough. She thought Daddy should let me have more fun since she never had any growing up. Well Mike offered to help me out. We arranged for him to call Daddy and ask if he could take me out. Daddy knew Mike's family from many years back. Daddy and Mike's father had worked at Studebaker's together before Mike's father started working for the South Bend Tribune. Daddy knew Mike's "people," and so he gave him permission to take me out. We headed straight to Puddin's party.

Everyone was there and the party was live. There were cars lined up on both sides of the street leading up to Puddin's house. I don't know where her parents were, but nothing but good clean fun was going on as far as I could see. Just kids dancing. We danced until our hair "went back." We girls didn't have permanents in those days, just press and curl. One could easily sweat through the press unless there was a lot of grease on the curl. All of a sudden somebody said, "Steen here comes Rev Davis." "Oh my God." I was busted I thought. Someone shoved me and Mike into the hall coat closet just before Daddy knocked on the door. Puddin opened it. "Any y'all seen Teenie? "No, Rev Davis we haven't seen her, "said Puddin. "What about that Mike boy?" "No we haven't seen him either," Puddin replied. "Well, alright if you see Teenie tell her I was here." "Yes, Rev Davis, Good night," Puddin said closing the door. A few seconds later someone opened the closet door and said, "Hey Mike, Steen, the coast is clear, you can come out." The partying resumed in earnest. To this day I do not know how that man could find out so much so quickly and track me down. It was as if he had one of those satellite tracking devices.

As soon as the party was over and we stepped out into the cool night air and things heated up again. There sitting right in front of Puddin's house was—you guessed it, "The Rev" there to take me safely home. "Daddy, you've embarrassed me," I fumed. He threw back his head and laughed as he gripped the steering wheel guiding the Buick onto Washington Street and said, "You'd a really been embarrassed if I'd a whipped yo behind. Teenie, You go'n learn. You go'n learn." I did begin to learn and began to see the lessons that Dad was trying to teach me, especially as I saw several more girls drop out of school pregnant, some of them were very smart— in the books. I was not going to be in that number and my junior prom would prove to be a major test for me.

I asked a guy named John, a good looking, popular basketball player, who was also a member of the Top Cats, to my junior prom. My good friend Brenda went with Ben, Recie went with Beverly, and Mike took Connie; whom I hated with a purple passion and for no reason. Connie had never done anything to me or said anything about me. It was as if I had assigned to her the label arch enemy. The real problem was that she had two things I wanted, she was a cheerleader, and she was a light brown complexion. In later years I made peace with myself about her. I don't know that she ever knew how much I disliked her. The point of fact was I was simply envious.

Back to the prom. Now I don't think any of the guys really wanted to be with any of us, but they couldn't very well take the white girls they were dating. We all went to the prom which was uneventful. Afterwards, I think they took us to some really cheap place like McDonald's to eat; saving their money apparently for the motel out on Western Avenue. Mike and Recie were in one room with Beverly and Connie; John and I along with Brenda and Ben were in another room. Their game plan was to "shake a tail feather"—as the jargon was to "score" or have their way with us. While John and I did some serious kissing, there was no way he was ever going to get past my girdle. Seeing how he wanted to go all the way, I joined Brenda in the rest room, where she was sitting on the toilet with the lid closed reading a magazine, and leaving Ben totally frustrated that he couldn't even score a good kiss. We were not going to become their bragging rights.

The next Monday, however, I ran into Donald and he looked at me with a disgusted expression on his face as we passed in the hall. "Donald what's wrong with you?" I said. He replied, "I thought you were a better girl than that," "What are you talking about?" I asked. Donald then went on to tell me that John was bragging about "shaking a tail feather" with me. I was furious because my reputation was now on the line. Recie is the only person I could get on the phone that Monday evening. I asked Recie if it were true that John was saying he had sex with me. Recie wouldn't confirm nor deny it, except to say he didn't believe John. That was all the answer I needed. I could not wait to get to school the next day. I waited under the big clock where we all gathered each day at Central. I soon saw John walking toward me alone. I confronted him. "Did you say you shook a tail feather with me? You know nothing happened." "No Steen, I know nothing happened, you know I wouldn't say anything like that about you," said John. About that time, Hardy and Ben walked up, John completely changed his tune in front of the guys and said, "You know what we did!" I drew back to slug him a good right cross the chin, but Hardy caught my arm just before my punch landed. "Steen you can't be fighting a boy here in school." I stopped speaking to John for an entire year. Finally one day I ran into him downtown just before he graduated and he apologized. Years later when he got married, he brought his wife by to meet me and said to her, "I want you to meet a real lady. If I hadn't married you, it would have been her." I felt vindicated. Delay doesn't mean denial.

"The mills of God grind slowly, yet they grind exceeding small,"

—Friedrich Von Logau

The rest of my junior and senior years were fairly

uneventful—except in November, 1963. About mid-morning we were passing classes at Central, when the announcement that shattered our world came over the PA system. "President John. F. Kennedy has been shot and has been pronounced dead out in Dallas, Texas." This was my President, Camelot. I wanted my mother to name my younger sister "Jacqueline" after the First Lady. Instead Mom named her Mae Rose, how unsophisticated was that?

The Kennedy's were the beautiful, sophisticated, committed first couple. President Kennedy and his brother sent the troops down south so that kids could go to school together—as we so took for granted in the north. I was devastated. Two of my white friends, Helene and Gail happened along, and we just hugged and cried. In between sobs, I said "every time someone comes along who wants to help black people, they are killed." When I got home, Daddy was glued to the TV. It would be the first time I'd ever see him cry. Tears were rolling down his cheeks. He just stared at the set. I was living through a time of irreversible change and loss of innocence in the United States. To see the pictures of little John-

127

John saluting his father was just simply heart breaking.

One light moment occurred when Daddy, forever the comedian, remarked about how composed Jackie Kennedy was in the public eye. Daddy said you could always tell when a widow was left well off, they just dabbed at their eyes and were thankful that they were left in such good stead. He said the ones who weren't left any money, and were trying to figure out how they were going to pay for the funeral, were the ones who would be wailing and hollering, "Oh John, why did you have to leave me?" Daddy continued, "what you didn't hear is how she finished that question under her breath—with all these bills and no money." Daddy could be incredibly funny and bring light to almost any situation.

The Tri-Alphas occupied a lot of my time. It felt good to be a member of this all–important group which was made up of the *crème de la crème* of young women at Central. But the hurt would come again. Most of my fellow members of Tri-Alpha were chosen as debutantes for the Alpha Kappa Alpha sorority—

I wasn't. It wasn't my grades, they were really good. Perhaps it was my reputation as a brawler. It didn't matter that I was fighting for my very survival, I thought. The people who started the fights would never be involved in much of anything. They only wanted to drag you down with them. In too many instances, I allowed that to happen—because the fleas come with the dog.

"You can be ever so smart, but don't let your achievements take you to a place your character can't reach."

—*Unknown*

For my Senior Prom I took Al from Washington High School. He picked me up in his uncle's white and red convertible Ford Thunderbird. Al wore a plaid tuxedo jacket and I had on a beautiful princess cut pink gown. We were quite the couple. Al was a drop dead handsome football star. Al's mother adored me as I did her. She was a wonderfully sweet woman. For Christmas one year, I gave her a standing ceramic dachshund cup holder. She

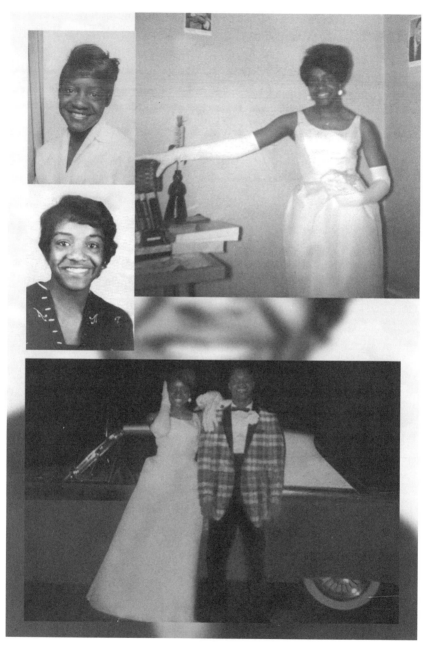

Senior Prom

kept it on display in her kitchen for years. Sadly, her son did not share his mother's adoration for me. He broke up with me for a fair-skinned cheerleader from the East Side and I was crushed. We reap what we sow. She later dumped him for a rich white guy who she later married.

Daddy and I would have one more battle of the wills before college. I had told him for graduation I was really going to "tie one on." I don't think he knew what I was talking about because he just laughed but if he did know what I was talking about I'm sure he thought surely I was joking.

The Central High school graduation ceremony was held on June 4, 1964, in the evening at Washington High School in their gym. As we marched into the gymnasium to the strains of *Pomp and Circumstance*, Mom said Dad swelled with pride and tears welled up in his eyes. She said when they called my name during the awarding of Diplomas, the tears rolled down his cheeks and he said, "Go'n Teenie. Go'n Teenie."

High School Graduation

Chapter Five

College Bound

It was the second time I ever heard tell of my Daddy crying. These were tears of pride and joy. By the grace of God, he was able to safely guide his first–born through the hurdles of a changing society, a clash of cultures, and a strong-willed woman-child, who was the mirror image of himself. She was graduating from high school, she wasn't pregnant, and she was going off to college!

By this time, we had moved to a much nicer home. Dad had rebounded financially and had purchased a couple rental properties. I'd often go and collect rent with him. But it was graduation time and time for the party of all parties to be held at my house. Black kids, white kids, nearly everyone in the graduating class converged on my house; It was packed. About 11:30 p.m., I left to get some booze. I can't recall who was buying it for us because we were all under age. By the time I got back, Rev had come home and I wasn't there—to all of these drunken seniors. Daddy bellowed, "This party is over, y'all go home." He proceeded to put everyone out. I came back slightly tipsy; I told Dad I was going to get drunk. He said all right if you want to drink, I'll be right back. He got a fifth of vodka and sat me down. "Drink," he said until you've had enough and then clean these floors. I was expected to dust mop and wax the hardwood floors that my friends had scuffed up. I could have had an alcohol overdose, I was so sick. Never again I vowed. I think sometimes Daddy got a kick out of making me miserable.

One evening during the summer, before I left for college, Dad said, "Teenie come here, read this". There in the newspaper was a picture of Rena and her cousin Shirley getting arrested for prostitution. It was Shirley's mother who thought Daddy was too strict and should relax the rules more. I immediately saw the point he was trying to make. Everything was becoming clearer. Other lessons also became crystal clear, when I was riding through downtown and saw this girl, her mother, and her grandmother standing in the line for people to collect food stamps and government cheese. Three generations on the dole. In hindsight, Daddy wasn't so strict after all. I even realized that I might have been a tad spoiled.

My Daddy wanted me to go to Spelman College in Atlanta. I didn't know anything about Spelman and no one in my circle of friends had ever gone there or knew anyone who had gone there. I had heard about Howard, where one of my friend's was going, but everyone said I would be socially ostracized there because of my skin color. Was I ever going to get away from this color nonsense? Color was never an issue among whites when I was younger. It was among my own race that color appeared to always be an issue. The dark-skinned black guys wanted light-skinned or white girls. The light-skinned boys' families wanted them to keep the color line and not taint it with a darker hue. What was a dark-skinned girl to do? My fair-skinned Aunt said we should stay with our own kind. Whew! Among us African Americans there is so much pathos.

Since Howard wasn't an option and Spelman was someplace I nor my counselors had ever heard of, my first choice became Marquette University in Wisconsin, a very prestigious Catholic University where Bruce, my friend Pam's boyfriend attended. We couldn't afford the out-of-state tuition for Marquette, so I settled for Ball State Teachers College in Muncie where my good friend Charles had gone—Ball State is now a University. I majored in Business Education with a minor in English. My full intention was to teach business education. My fees were $98 dollars a quarter. Daddy gave me my money as I was preparing to leave. I carefully rolled and tied it up in a handkerchief. Daddy said don't lose that money, as I was depositing it in my bosom like I'd seen Aunt Mary do. When I said I was putting it in my bra, Daddy laughed and said you're sure to lose it now. He just laughed, but he was so proud; Teenie was going to college.

Off to college I went—on the bus, with my big black trunk. Mom nor Dad went with me because they had no experience with such things. I felt a little put out when I saw the white families bringing their children to the dorm and helping them move in. My roommate for orientation was a white girl from a small southern Indiana town. Her parents immediately requested a transfer for her and got it. I ended up moving off campus to a rooming house run by a lady named Mrs. Moore. She was a very large, cheery woman married to a man with big horsey teeth. When he smiled, which was often, Mr. Moore looked like a donkey. Mrs. Moore had six of us girls at her house and she watched us like a hawk; often threatening to call Rev. Davis on me when I broke curfew.

Mom dutifully sent me $5 a week for food which lasted about three days. Why not get a job?

Where? How would I get there with no transportation? This was the first time I didn't have what I needed and seemingly no one to help. For starters, the counselors didn't feel we black students should be going to college in the first place. Secondly, blacks in positions to help shared no information except for the elite few. I didn't even fill out the financial aid form because I didn't think or know that I needed it.

With all the children in my family, we'd grown from four to nine, I could have been eligible for all kinds of grants and aid. Instead, Daddy was paying my way and my siblings were complaining bitterly. Every time I came home my brothers especially were carping that all the money was going to me and they didn't have anything. None of this sat very well with me, always the proud one. I rarely had enough money to take care of basics and I didn't know how to maneuver the system because my mind-set was not one of need. I never needed anything in my life. But here I was an above average student without the basics for getting my education. I just expected that I would have what I needed, just as it had always been. Daddy had shared with us that he planned to sell off his rental properties to fund college for each of the four older children. That plan had long since fallen apart with Studebaker's closing and five more children to feed. He had to sell the houses.

I have to admit my priorities were as mixed up as a tossed salad. I barely had money for room and board, no money for books, or incidentals; and yet, I still wanted a new coat for homecoming. I sent Daddy a postcard asking for money for the coat. Daddy wrote back to me, *"No money. Too bad, so sad—your Dad."* I was livid. So this spoiled brat packed her things, quit school, and came home. I vowed to earn my own way. I was a college dropout. Daddy was so disappointed, but there was nothing much he could do now. He had taken me as far as he could and the rest would be up to me.

For about one week, I baby sat for a white family who lived across the street. Despite having diapered half my siblings, I wasn't ready for the foul–smelling diaper duty I encountered one day. I think it was a matter of knowing I could do better than just baby–sit. That experience led me to feel that the cute little baby had the worst smelling poop I had ever encountered. I quit that very day and immediately applied at the Associates Corporation, where I was hired as a secretary.

Chapter Six

Love & Marriage

My business education skills paid handsome dividends. I could type at 70 to 80 words per minute and take shorthand at about 120 wpm. The bonus was I had excellent written and verbal communication skills. It wasn't long before I was promoted to be trained on the IBM magnetic tape Selectrix typewriter, the forerunner of the personal computer. It was a great job with great pay. I had started dating a guy named Percy who was in the Air Force. My family adored him. His family was fond of me as well. It was a foregone conclusion that we would be married and we were unofficially engaged. I didn't have a ring. Percy was brown skinned and nice looking, a first–class gentleman, who treated me like a Queen. I liked him a lot and Daddy trusted him implicitly. He and Daddy had long, long talks. Percy's family and mine had much in common. Both families' roots were in Mississippi and they were hard working, decent church going people. Percy's family was one of the first black families to build their own home from the ground up in the early sixties! In fact, it was featured in the homes section of the South Bend Tribune. They were really great people and Miss Luberta, Percy's mom, was one of my role models. We enjoyed shopping together and I got her recipe for the killer pecan pies she made.

Daddy tried to protect Percy's interest and would insist there were still places I could not go. One evening I was devastated because here I was 19 years old and still couldn't go skating. Daddy's favorite line was let people miss you. Don't be common and have people expect to see you at everything. I could not go skating. Furious, I walked down the street to the St. Joe River. As I looked out of the corner of my eye I could see Daddy driving along slightly behind me. I stopped and stood at the railing looking at the swirling waters of the river. Daddy yelled out of the car window, "jump, Teenie, jump..." and started laughing. Always the drama queen, I spun around and stormed back down the street to the house. Dad, of course, had beat me home, called my best friend Karen, who was engaged to Percy's brother Darlies, and told her she'd better talk to her friend because I looked like I was about to jump into the river! I thank God that I was not an emotionally fragile person. His risky reverse psychology certainly worked. On yet another occasion, I was standing over the sink with a bottle of aspirin, saying, "I can't take it anymore. Goodbye cruel world." Before I could get the bottle of aspirin open, Dad came out of his bedroom with a vial of medicine and said, "Here take a couple of these, they'll kick you right out of here." I wanted to scream. Instead, I stormed up the stairs to my bedroom and boo–hooed. This man never stopped and he thought it was hilarious to play mind games with me. He was indeed watching me for Percy.

But along came LeRoy King, six years my senior, just out of the Air Force and a computer whiz. He was gorgeous, smart, well-dressed, and light skinned with "good" hair, just the kind of man my grandmother and great grandmother would approve of—and interested in me! His younger brother Jon or "Sugar" as we called him, and I were high school buddies but I never knew LeRoy since he was away. LeRoy would later tell me that when he saw me walking down the street from school, he decided I would be his wife.

LeRoy and I started dating. The only problem was LeRoy, who had been married before with two children, was dating a couple other people, both of whom had gotten pregnant. The law was looking for him to slap him with paternity suits. He swore to me that these children were not his. I believed him and defied my parents and friends to stay with him. I'll never forget one evening LeRoy was bringing me home and Daddy was waiting for us on the front porch. Daddy said, "Son, as a personal favor to me would you please leave my daughter alone?" LeRoy's first wife Cynthia was the daughter of one of Daddy's good friends and LeRoy and Cynthia had two children. Daddy made it clear that even though I had nothing to do with their breakup, as long as they had children together, they were still married under the sight of God. Mom was not speaking biblically but put it bluntly, "You don't need to marry someone with a ready–made family." The relationship did not have my parent's blessings.

But finally a gorgeous, accomplished guy was interested in chocolate me. LeRoy's Aunt told me not to marry her nephew but to go back to school because he was just like her brother. LeRoy also had two children by a girl from Bermuda while he was in the Air Force. None of this mattered to me, I was in love with a capital "L." Birds were singing in my head and hearts covered my eyes. Since there was so much heat with all the questions of paternity, LeRoy decided to move to Washington, D.C. I decided I wanted to go as well, but had planned to live with Barbara, a friend who had already moved there.

LeRoy & Steen

When I told my folks that I was moving to D.C. and was going to ride there with LeRoy, Daddy said, "ya'll might as well get married." It was arranged, Rev. Williams, a long–time family friend, would perform the ceremony. We would get married in the living room. Mom was so upset she left home and didn't return, complaining as she left out the door that her first–born was getting married like a thief in the night. Now Mom could fuss, but I'd never seen her so angry. Again I would see my Daddy cry. LeRoy's Dad, "Buckshot" came and the nuptials were held. After Rev. Williams pronounced us man and wife, he said the strangest thing... "What's done in the dark will come to the light." It dawned on me that they all thought I was pregnant. I wasn't, as God is my witness. I just was not about to let LeRoy get away and I was more than ready to leave South Bend.

Sanctify them through thy truth: thy word is truth
(John, 17:17)

LeRoy and I got married on February 12, 1966, which was four days before Percy was scheduled to be discharged from the Air Force. His mom saw the license notice in the newspaper and called to find out whether it was true. Sadly, Daddy said it was. Miss Luberta said she wasn't going to tell Percy until she picked him up at the airport. Needless to say, Percy was devastated. He sat for days with my Dad and sometimes broke into tears asking "Why." I didn't even have the decency to write him a "Dear John" letter, he had to find out when he got home, thinking he would put a ring on my finger.

Be not deceived; God is not mocked:
for whatsoever a man soweth, that shall he also reap.
(Galatians, 6:7)

The trip to D.C. detoured to Cincinnati where we were to visit one of LeRoy's Air Force buddies, Tom and his wife Barbara. What was to have been a stop in Cincinnati—en route to Washington, D.C., resulted in our staying in the city of seven hills for nearly two years.

A few months after getting married I made my first visit home. I went to church wearing one of those tunic tops that was popular at the time. One of the ladies in the church lifted up my top to pat at my stomach, which was flat as a pancake. I said to her "no ma'am, I'm not pregnant." It would be two years before I got pregnant. Dad even started bugging me about when he was going to get a grand baby. I told him I had to see how this man was going to act before I started having a bunch of children.

During our time in Cincinnati, I took a civil service test for the Agency for International Development. I got the highest score in the five state Ohio region and was offered a job in D.C., I turned down the offer. I was too concerned about the ratio of women to men and worried about the women in the District taking my husband! Can you imagine that? I worked as a Division secretary for General Electric. I was appointed by the Chamber of Commerce as a sort of an executive on loan to help set up the Opportunities Industrialization Center (OIC) in Cincinnati where I taught business education, the use of office machines, and shorthand. I would take my first plane ride to Philadelphia to meet the founder of the OIC, the Rev. Leon Sullivan. I was pregnant by now and at the fancy cocktail party, all I could think about was Rice Krispies and strawberries.

LeRoy, who was a computer whiz, had received an offer to return to South Bend with the Bendix Corporation. They wanted him so desperately they offered me a job at their Mishawaka office, a suburb of South Bend 15 miles away. We jumped at the chance to return home, especially since things had quieted down regarding his paternity problems. One girl had moved out of town and the other girl married someone who took on the child as his. Our first born came into the world on a Sunday afternoon, April 21, 1968. She was due on April 4th and since that was the date of Martin Luther King's Assassination, I had thought if she were a girl I'd name her Martina King. I'd eaten some collard greens the Saturday night before and you know the folklore, collard greens will indeed cause you to go into labor—if you're late. That Sunday morning my water broke and the contractions started coming closer and closer together. LeRoy was out of town with my brother-in-law Eugene, retrieving the rest of our furnishings in Cincinnati. My mother-in-law, Ma King (Inez) drove me to the hospital and was met by Mom. Dad peeked in for a moment before having to head off to 11 o'clock service. I have always been conscious of my appearance and had painstakingly applied my makeup, fixed my hair with my fall—a half wig held together with a hair band—before we left for the hospital; I was frustrating my mother-in-law who did not want me to have that baby on her. When those labor pains started getting harder and more difficult, I snatched that wig off and got down to business, not caring what I looked like. The birth was without consequence and I delivered a healthy baby girl, who Mom said looked just like me. I was crushed. Since I didn't think much of my looks, I immediately thought, "I've got an ugly baby." We named her Kellie, with the middle name Jo, for LeRoy's sister Constance Jo; who had been so sweet to me. I was told Kellie was the prettiest child born in that hospital that year. The nurses took their time bringing her to me and kept walking around St. Joseph's Hospital showing her off.

Daddy was ecstatic. He had his first born grandchild. A little girl who he said looked like Mom, when he knew all along the strong Davis genes were showing in her face. Daddy would come over and launch into lessons about how to teach her how to speak correct English and the child was barely out of the womb! Oh how he loved that little girl.

Labor Day weekend, Daddy wanted to take her around to visit some family friends before he left on another of his trips. Mom wouldn't let him take her because it was getting chilly and little Kellie didn't have a sweater at the house. She didn't know it would be the last time Daddy would see his beloved granddaughter.

Chapter Seven

The Fourth Day of the Month

The year 1968 would see the loss of two giants, one nationally renowned, the other well known in South Bend, Indiana. When Dr. Martin Luther King, Jr. was assassinated in Memphis, it would be the fourth time I would see my Dad cry. The third time was at the funeral for his younger brother, Rev. Floyd Davis who died of a stroke at 43 in Cincinnati. My Uncle Floyd and a young minister by the name of

Rev. Moss were both "sons" of Rev. Edmundson of First Baptist Church in Cincinnati. I had never before and rarely since heard a preacher as eloquent as Rev. Moss.

Uncle Floyd's death was a painful lesson to me. He was a dapper, but not flashy, Cadillac driving minister of the gospel—who was fun. He didn't miss an opportunity to tell me how Dad had spoiled me. I wondered what was in those Camel cigarettes he smoked if he thought I was spoiled! Uncle Floyd had a stroke one Sunday in the pulpit. When Aunt Naomi phoned, I thought, "he's in the hospital, I'll go visit him tomorrow." Tomorrow was too late. Unfortunately, Uncle Floyd died that Sunday night and I didn't get a chance to see him.

Lesson: Never put off for tomorrow what you can do today because it is not promised to you. The death of his brother (friend) was especially hard on Daddy, but the death of Dr. Martin Luther King sat him down in front of the TV for days. He listened to the news commentators and watched the events unfolding in Memphis and Atlanta. Daddy had an opportunity to meet Dr. King and visit with him when Dr. King swung over to South Bend from Chicago. Dr. King met and had lunch with members of the South Bend Ministerial Alliance. It was a high point in Daddy's life, which would end, five months to the day of Dr. King's death. Daddy drove Army trucks made at the Kaiser Jeep plant for delivery to various Army posts. He was always trying to make certain he took care of his family. Mom worked to get the "frills," not because she had to, he always provided the basics. Daddy left that weekend to deliver two trucks to Fort Campbell in Kentucky—driving one truck with the other sitting piggy back on the one he was driving.

On Wednesday morning, September 4, 1968, I could not get started. I seemed out of focus and felt that something was wrong, I just couldn't put my finger on it. Auntie, Dad's Aunt Mary, cared for my Kellie while LeRoy and I worked. I called her to see if Kellie was ok. She was. I called Mom, she was fine. I dismissed the foreboding feeling as fatigue from a Labor Day weekend of backyard barbecuing. Around 10:30 in the morning, a colleague

The Ministerial Alliance

came to my office telling me that my mother had phoned and said to call home. I thought it was strange since I had spoken with her earlier and everything was ok. I went on to lunch and was playing cards with some co–workers, when Aunt Mary's niece, by marriage, came into the cafeteria and said forcefully, "Steen you need to go home, something has happened." She went on to say, "they've taken your mother to the hospital." LeRoy, in the meantime, was driving to lunch and heard the bulletin on the radio:

"Longtime South Bend resident, Rev. Austin Davis,
was killed in a one-vehicle crash in
Southern Indiana early today..."

LeRoy began speeding toward Mishawaka to get to me before I heard it on the radio or from someone else. For some strange reason I didn't turn on the radio as I headed home to Mom's house. I began to think why they would want me to go to the house if they had to take Mom to the hospital? Which hospital? It hit me, nothing is wrong with

Mom—It's Dad. LeRoy had dreamed a couple weeks prior that Daddy had been in a bad wreck and that he had been killed. When I drove up to our house on Colfax, just a few blocks down the street from Notre Dame, I saw the state trooper cruisers and Rev. White standing at the front door. I just starting shaking my head, crying, what happened to my Daddy? I threw the car in park and ran to the door. Rev. White met me and spoke words that cut to the marrow. "There was a bad accident, Teenie, your Daddy is gone home to be with the Lord." The pain from those words emanated from the bowels of my belly. The tire rod had broken on the truck Dad was driving. He apparently lost control and the truck went over a steep ravine. Police say he died instantly. It was an indescribable anguish that only God himself could soothe. I cried out, "God, No!"

Death is so final. There was no chance to prepare. It came out of nowhere. Work undone was left undone. My Daddy was only 47 years old, a good man, who was the anchor—not only for our nuclear family, but for our extended family and many in the community. My sister

<u>Come Go With Me</u>

He came one morning early and said to him,
come go with me.

The man replied you know I can't, I have a
family.

To come I know is against your will as it is
with everyone.
But my dear son, your work on earth is done.

I'll be a father to your children
and tell them not to cry.

Because one day they will join you
in your box seat on high.

—Teenie

Mary, who was entering college the next couple weeks, was totally distraught. The last words she had spoken to Dad were that she hated him because he wouldn't let her go wherever it was she wanted to go. Rev. White tried to assure her that Daddy knew she was only speaking in the heat of the moment. It was to no avail. She was inconsolable. We worried about her for months when she went off to college. Richard was equally devastated. The star basketball player was entering his all important senior year. He could always look up into the stands and count on Dad being there. Who would help him make his college choices and keep him on the straight and narrow? Little Darlies, the knee-baby (next to the last child), who was the spitting image of Dad; grabbed Dad's briefcase and hat refusing to allow anyone to touch them. At five years of age, he was hurt and angry.

There was no question that Mr. Clark, a long-time family friend, who owned Clark's Funeral Home, would handle the funeral. I helped my mother go through all the necessary motions of funeral arrangements, which included pulling together Dad's obituary and laying out his favorite black suit. We picked out a copper casket with praying hands at the four corners. It was all so surreal, like a dream—a bad dream. I kept expecting to wake up and that Daddy would again bound through the front door, virtually ignoring me and LeRoy with a few brief hellos, and asking, "Where's the baby?"

I Remember

The girl laughed at another little girl
who was ragged and sad
The man said, "Remember daughter, there but by
the grace of God, walketh I."
I Remember

Dignified, dejected, intelligent, resourceful,
Tall in stature, short in the world of lesser men
Humanitarian, tall black and proud
I Remember

A fighter, a teacher, a humorist, full of love.
Without his guidance, where might I have fallen?
Fought a losing battle, wounded from mortal blows.
Falling, fell, time running out.
Leaving loved ones
September 4, I Remember

—Teenie

New Salem Baptist, a mega-church by 1960 standards seated 500 people. The sanctuary was filled to capacity the day of the service. There were no seats in the basement and people were standing two deep outside. Everyone from the Congressman and Mayor; to the Chapin Street drunks were there. Ten ministers provided "Echo's from the Field," they were Daddy's best friends; Rev. Kirk and Rev. White; his mentor Rev. Rowlette; Rev. West, the other Rev. Davis; Daddy's Pastor, Rev. Johnson, Rev. Byrd, Rev. Shead; Rev. Berry, and Rev. Crockett. Daddy was extremely well-known and respected. Brother Morell, Rev. Dave Davis' son-in-law, had been brought into the church by Dad. He struggled to keep his tears in check as he lifted his melodious baritone and sang,

"Precious Lord take my hand, lead me on let me stand..."

My mind ran a video of all the crazy things I had done, how utterly disobedient I had been. Why was I such a maverick? Why didn't I go to Spelman?

Why did I drop out of college? Why did I break Percy's heart? Why, Why, Why? Yet though I stumbled, I had the blessed assurance that my earthly and heavenly Father loved me enough to never give up on me. Daddy went to his grave knowing that even though I chose to do things my own way, I did not dishonor him or myself. Daddy also knew that I loved and respected him because fortunately I had matured to the point that I did thank him on several occasions for his tough love and guidance.

I was making it through the funeral and could even smile at some of the remembrances and remarks made by the parade of eulogists. It would be selfish of me to want Daddy to stay here following the accident. He would have been a vegetable with the massive head injuries he'd suffered. God was merciful and I was working through my grief toward acceptance. But, midway through the service the unexpected happened. The funeral attendants started closing the casket. As long as Daddy's body was in view, I was coping. I utterly lost control when they started to slowly crank down the lid. "No!" I screamed, sobbing uncontrollably as I attempted to climb over the usher sitting next to me at the end of the pew. "Please let me see my Daddy one more time, please!" I desperately wanted to get one last look at him to touch him; but several strong arms including those of my husband LeRoy, restrained me with such force I seemed to gasp frantically for air. Twenty-two years of training ended at New Salem Baptist Church, on a crisp fall Tuesday, in South Bend, Indiana.

Pitifully, all I could moan was *"Daddy!"*

Teenie: Newslady in Training

Epilogue

For several weeks after the funeral, I went to Dad's grave site. While there was not yet a headstone, I had no trouble finding it. It was just past the Studebaker mausoleum at City Cemetery. I would sit there and cry for hours. Sometimes I just sat. I was beginning to make myself sick and needed to get a hold of myself. Daddy was gone in the physical, but he would always be with me in the spiritual. Just as Jesus told the disciples, I will leave you a comforter. My comfort came in the form of a pearl that my Aunt Alberta shared with me, "As long as you live, your father will be with you." I've come to understand that one of God's truly great gifts is memory. We always have those wonderful memories of our loved ones. The greatest legacy my father instilled in me was Love of God, Love of Self, Love of Family, and Love of Community. My charge is to model his example and be the woman he trained me to be. God knows he tried and so do I.

Steen on Set

Today "Teenie" is called Steen Miles the "Newslady." She is an Emmy-award winning broadcast journalist—considered a pioneer among African Americans in the field. She was the first African American female television news reporter in South Bend, Indiana. After 30 years in broadcasting, in 2005, Steen Miles was elected to the Georgia Senate and served a two-year term before seeking the Democratic nomination for Lieutenant Governor of Georgia, polling third among five candidates. Senator Miles is a sought after speaker who has spoken to audiences all over the United States in the Caribbean, South Korea, and the Holy Land. She has been invited to the White House twice, the recipient of dozens of journalism awards; along with hundreds of civic awards and commendations. She is a passionate advocate for families, women, and youth. The mother of two accomplished adult daughters and two grandchildren. Senator Miles is an associate minister at the Greenforest Community Baptist Church, located in Decatur, Georgia.

Train up a child in the way that he should go and when he is old, he will not depart from it.

(Proverbs, 22:6)

"To God be the glory for all that he has done!"

-Steen Miles

Acknowledgements

This book would not have been possible without the love and support of my First Lady, Dr. Sadie Turner McCalep, owner of Orman Press and the wife of my late Pastor, Dr. George O. McCalep, Jr., of the Greenforest Community Baptist Church in Decatur, Georgia. Pastor McCalep began Orman Press to publish his own works and give voice to struggling authors who might otherwise not be in print. Dr. Sadie T. McCalep continues his legacy.

My sincere thanks also to Sandra Ferguson and Sarah Reid for their technical expertise, patience, and loving critiques. Finally, heartfelt thanks to Bishop Jim Swilley, Pastor of the Church In The Now of Conyers, Georgia and relationship expert Dr. Joyce Morley Ball for taking time out of their busy schedules to review this work.

Always thanks be to God for He is good!

Stay tuned for...

The Newslady!